PROGRAMMING
My Mind for Success

Dr Piers Finesse

authorHOUSE®

AuthorHouse™
1663 Liberty Drive
Bloomington, IN 47403
www.authorhouse.com
Phone: 1 (800) 839-8640

© 2018 Dr Piers Finesse. All rights reserved.

No part of this book may be reproduced, stored in a retrieval system, or transmitted by any means without the written permission of the author.

bible citations: Scripture taken from The Holy Bible, King James Version. Public Domain

Published by AuthorHouse 08/27/2018

ISBN: 978-1-5462-5340-2 (sc)
ISBN: 978-1-5462-5339-6 (e)

Library of Congress Control Number: 2018908931

Print information available on the last page.

Any people depicted in stock imagery provided by Getty Images are models, and such images are being used for illustrative purposes only.
Certain stock imagery © Getty Images.

This book is printed on acid-free paper.

Because of the dynamic nature of the Internet, any web addresses or links contained in this book may have changed since publication and may no longer be valid. The views expressed in this work are solely those of the author and do not necessarily reflect the views of the publisher, and the publisher hereby disclaims any responsibility for them.

CONTENTS

Acknowledgement vii
Introduction ix
1) As a man thinks 1
2) Expanding your mind 5
3) A New Mind 12
4) Strongholds of the Mind 17
5) The Limited Mind 21
6) The Visionary's Mind 27
7) A Transformed Mind 31
8) Imaginations of the mind 34
9) The negative mind 38
10) The mindset 53
11) Think BIG 58
12) A focused mind 64
13) The mind and speaking 72
14) Destiny-minded 78
15) Business-minded 81
16) Generational thinking 88
17) Thinking outside the box 92
18) A mind to work 97
19) The progressive mind 102
20) Grasshopper mentality 108
21) Programming the mind 115
22) Think on purpose 122
23) Declarations 129

Biography 137

ACKNOWLEDGEMENT

I dedicate this book to my wife Grace Finesse, my two daughters, Blessing and Bethany, and my son Bryden. Pursue your purposes with all the effort you can muster. I love you all.

Total and sincere expression of my gratitude to all my siblings and their wives for making the production of this book possible.

Thanks to Attorney Elisha Finesse and my College Lecturer Kenneth Gwena for proof-reading my manuscript.

This book is being given

to..

By..

"Beware of what you think, you eventually become an embodiment of your obsessive thoughts" Dr Piers Finesse.

"You cannot have a positive life and a negative mind" Joyce Meyer

INTRODUCTION

A story is told of two fish, one born in a pond and the other in the sea. While at a certain meeting, the two argued about the preeminence of their backgrounds. Amazingly the fish born in a pond thought the pond was larger than the sea. Of course, there is more water in a sea than there is in a pond, and a pond is just a body of standing water, either natural or artificial, that is usually smaller than a lake. Exposure may affect the way we decipher, assimilate, interpret and deduce information.

A study done by the University of Pennsylvania showed that the number of young people addicted to gambling increased due to exposure to Internet gambling. The numbers grew by a startling 20 % between 2004 and 2005 alone. We define life relative to our exposure and experiences. Bigger experiences take on life with a wider perspective and spectrum. But thank God we can increase the borders of our exposure and hence extend our mindsets. It has never ceased to amaze me when composing a song just how it can have so many variations in terms of the lyrics, music, backing vocals and so forth. A set of the same words given to different people can bring up many different songs.

Life is not limited to a few, little and meager options. Your mind will adopt to the new situation and innovate. The mind is limitless unless limited by you. There are countless possibilities with your name on them. Seize, occupy and possess them. You are destined for greatness. The mind can adapt, adjust and change to meet the new requirements of thought-processing. It's amazing what the mind can do. Widen your world.

Programming is vital for the mind to carry out specific instructions that will result in desired behavior and lifestyle. A negatively programmed mind will run amok and hence produce weird behavior, speech and conduct. Philippians 4v8 says, "think ye upon these things". Think ye upon these things is a definition of programming. Stamp pure thoughts on the conscious and subconscious or subjective mind and they will become a reality.

The mind must be told what to process or it will process anything by default. Choose to live by design and not default. Your mind is a processor and will work on what comes in it. Feed it with material that will elevate and promote your life. We need to methodically, systematically and gradually debug and correct our minds so that we can go towards a desired path. Our minds should be cleansed and sanctified by the word of God as seen in John 17v17.

Change your thoughts and your increase will come. Don't waste time in past failures or future fantasies, take life by the horns today. Do something strategic and deliberate to alter your thinking process daily. Your daily habits will dictate your destiny. Don't be surprised by your end because you are contributing to it right now. Bit by bit, your daily thoughts are compounding into your future. The worst enemy is the one who damages your mind.

A damaged mind entails a damaged present and future. An abused mind will abuse others even without intention. A mind that is full of negative information will produce negative behavior. Think on things that are virtuous to create a virtuous life. A clogged mind will not produce as it ought to. Get rid of all contaminants and toxins that slow down the creativity in your mind. Have filters that grade the type of thoughts you accept or reject. What kind of seeds are you planting in the garden of your mind? Are you cultivating your mind? What kind of a harvest are you expecting from your thought life? Are you deliberate about your thoughts? The way you treat family, spouse, friends, relatives, workmates, classmates and people in general is predicated on your mind. What we think is of paramount importance-if you think you are poor then you are. Find a way to inject positive and life-giving thoughts to yourself. Do yourself a favor.

CHAPTER ONE

AS A MAN THINKS

"A mind grows by what it feeds on" *J. G. Holland*

Proverbs 23:7: (For as he thinketh in his heart, so is he: Eat and drink, saith he to thee; but his heart is not with thee.)

God desires your success more than you do. God never created anybody or anything to fail. If you think you are a loser, then you are. If you think you are successful, then you are. You gravitate towards your controlling, domineering and strongest thoughts. As you are all along in your thinking, so are you at last in your actions. Thinking is an inward reckoning.

As a man thinks so is he; you are a reflection of your thoughts. Nothing more, nothing less. What you conceive you can attain. Emancipation of the mind speaks volumes to the freedom of mankind. Even athletes believe that you win in the mind before winning a game. It starts in the mind. Our minds are different from each other, we need to cross-pollinate in order to tap and gain from other minds. We complete rather than compete with each other. The essence of cooperation is to bring all these varied and different minds to work for a common and one objective.

Within every human being is a mind. Within each mind is a belief system which molds us accordingly. Thoughts may come uninvited but you have the ultimate power to choose. We need a filter that separates good and bad thoughts. Change your thoughts and your world will change. Thoughts are so powerful that they cause physical reactions, for example, if you think you are ill-prepared for your academic examinations, your breathing rate races. You must think well and up. Thinking requires energy. You can't expand your living without expanding your thinking. Right thinking upgrades our lives.

3 John 1v2: (Beloved, I wish above all things that thou mayest prosper and be in health, even as thy soul prospers.)

Prosperity and health are related to the soundness of your mind. John wrote to his beloved, that he was desiring that they may prosper in all respects and be in good health, just as their souls were prospering. Success is predicated on the mindset. The successful and the unsuccessful are miles apart in their thinking processes. Be tired of the status-quo and train yourself in critical thinking because it is the highest paid skill. Mindsets affect our behaviors. A person's behavior is an outcome of their mindset. The mindset is like an escalator that takes you up or down. Choose to go up. Don't be influenced by the evil things around you but you should influence them, by the renewing of your mind.

A path of thinking leads to a pathway of life. Rebuild your mind. 90% of our thoughts are repeated daily unless if they are interrupted, disrupted, or confronted by a renewal message. These thoughts are subliminal, they are below the threshold of the conscious perception. The act of blaming and condemning others will not transform your pattern of thinking-take responsibility-answer the call for your thoughts. Your self-image or portrait in your mind needs to be changed because you attract and gain in accordance with that image. You attract who you are.

Your self-image is connected to your self-worth and net-worth. You are valuable in Christ. Let the mind of Christ master you. See yourself as God sees you. Your actions are a product of who you are. Who you are is equated to your mind. As a man thinketh, so is he.

Your mental framework or conceptual structure is fundamental to the direction that your life takes. Mental detoxification is a process of cleansing out your mind of toxic thoughts. It is necessary in order for your life to change. Defeat the thoughts of fear, condemnation and bitterness. Inject thoughts of success and think about them. Shift your way of thinking. Negative or positive thoughts are laid in us slowly but surely. The process is long and will surely affect our lifestyles eventually in a good or bad way. Don't allow weeds on the soil of your mind, be a diligent gardener. The devil is busy sowing tares but we need to remove them quickly.

Apostle Paul encourages us not to conform to current worldly and carnal surroundings. Our surroundings should not determine how we think. The way we think should be affected by the word and not the world. When we think according to the word then we can affect and influence our surroundings in a Godly manner. The surroundings can bring you down from your high position of authority in Christ if you allow their entrance.

Nowadays, movies are sending forth signals and messages that are worldly in order to tarnish our thinking patterns. We cannot reach a level that God desires for us until we change the way we think. We should not conform to the design or pattern of this world. Be careful of what you are placing before your eyes and ears because it enters your mind subliminally. Don't adapt to the ways of the world. Thoughts make or break you. About 90 % of all illnesses are a product of our thoughts. You are a summation of what you are conditioned to think. Condition yourself to think well. Our lives are corrupted when our thoughts revolve around devilish desires. That corruption leads to abuse of people, opportunities, gifts and talents. Our perspective of life is determined by the place from where we stand mentally. We don't see the world as it is but as we are.

Summary Points
- *A mind influenced by worldly patterns, instead of the word of God, is corrupted.*
- *Your mind can make or break you*
- *Your perspective of life is determined by the inclination of your mind.*
- *Direct your mind for progression and development*
- *Your mind is a vault packed with immense treasure*
- *Your life-style is a mirror of your thought-style*
- *You follow the path of your dominant thought*
- *A pathway of thinking leads to a pathway of life*
- *You are a product of your belief system*
- *An untrained mind can keep you hostage*
- *Your mind determines the size of your experiences*
- *A winning mind produces a winning life*
- *Thinking like a peasant closes doors to palaces*

CHAPTER TWO

EXPANDING YOUR MIND

"Books open your mind, broaden your mind, and strengthen you as nothing else can" *William Feather*

Isaiah 54v2:(Enlarge the place of thy tent, and let them stretch forth the curtains of thine habitations: spare not, lengthen thy cords, and strengthen thy stakes;)

The mind responds to training and exercise. The greatest asset you possess is the mind. Knowledge is your greatest investment. Knowledge brings light and helps you not to walk in darkness. It is not easy to unlearn what you have learned over a long time. It is better to be uneducated than to be wrongly educated. Learning is the secret behind the transformation of the mind-it stretches you. The yearning to learn should not diminish. You can't do better than you know-lengthen and widen the parameters of your mind. Be a student for the rest of your life. Life demands that we school ourselves daily in order to be updated than being outdated.

Not wanting to learn is an assumption that you have infinite knowledge. We live in a knowledge-based economy and what you learn determines what you earn. Learn to be a self-learner.

Self-learning is self-empowerment. Peter Daniels taught himself to read. Born in 1932 in Australia. Peter Daniels faced many difficulties, disadvantages and was associated with utter illiteracy in his early years. His family was third generation welfare recipients. His family was very dysfunctional. He failed at every grade in school and became a bricklayer. Failing is part of learning. To achieve more in life buy wisdom-buy books. About 130 million books have been published in the whole world. Develop a reading habit. Reading helps us to get ideas from the pages of a book. God left us a book-the bible. Study the word to show yourself as an approved workman. 50% of the people who complete and graduate from high school in the USA never finish reading a book in their life. When you stop learning, you stop growing. Learning and progress are directly related. Nobody has a monopoly on knowledge, you can learn as much as you want. No one can stop you from reading except you. Information costs but it pays for itself.

At 26 years of age, Peter Daniels was hopelessly in debt, and attended a Billy Graham Crusade on 25 May 1959. He attributes his life's change and subsequent success to that meeting. After reading about 2000 biographies, Daniels went into business three times, failing each time, but avoiding bankruptcy. Failure is an opportunity to start again. Winners fail until they succeed. Losers quit when they fail. He subsequently managed to build a large real estate business in Australia and South East Asia and serves as a director and chairman on a range of international boards. Daniels has been speaking on personal development for over thirty years. He is a life coach, writer, and professional speaker. Peter Daniels has authored thirteen books.

Surround yourself with an entourage of avid readers. Have your own library. Keep books that keep you on a path that you desire. Relearning can be difficult, but it is needed. Nothing just happens, so a deliberate move has to be taken towards personal continuing development and education. Listen to CD's and watch DVD'S that expand your thinking. Training strengthens the mind. One-hour CD per day is 365 hours of education per year, your life will change drastically. Reading is the aerobics of the mind. Reading compels the mind to think. Reading increases our world view. The orbit of the mind is enlarged. Reading a book transfers knowledge from one mind to another. What took someone 40 years to learn for a example can be gleaned from a book in a matter of hours-what an advantage. Reading will strengthen the mind just like bodily activity will do to the body. Myles Munroe reads a book every week. Abraham Lincoln was an avid reader. Warren Buffet reads between 500 and 1000 pages a day. Bill Gates is a ferocious reader. Bill Clinton is an omnivorous reader, in 1982, he read 300 books. Tai Lopez reads I book per day. Forbes reported that Chief Executive Officers read an average of two books per week. Persistence alone is not enough, you need to dress it with knowledge. Start to read a book today. Develop an appetite to be a ferocious and voracious reader. Readers lead. Readers write. Through reading you open up unknown worlds.

Advantages of reading
- *Alzheimer's probability is deflated.*
- *Verbal skills are refined.*
- *Stress is truncated.*
- *Imagination is improved.*
- *Knowledge is increased.*
- *Makes one smarter.*
- *Vocabulary is multiplied.*
- *Inspiration is upgraded.*
- *Memory is boosted.*
- *Analytical thinking skills are developed.*
- *Focus is sharpened.*
- *Writing skills are increased.*

Mental fitness is of paramount importance. So many secrets are hidden in books. Learn to accept productive thoughts, discard the unproductive ones-get rid of them. Life is not measured by what happens to you but by your response to those happenings. Think right. Think solutions. Think big. Think global. You can live in a bad environment and still control the environment of your mind just like an air-conditioned room. Creativity is related to quietness. In this hustle and bustle age, we can hardly find time to relax and create as it were. David would write the Psalms as he was shepherding the sheep in the quiet lands of Israel. He would create and compose exceptional and classical pieces of music. Have some quiet times. You will never falter in any venture that your mind is involved in wholly. Process those ideas and concepts thoroughly.

Blame shifting wastes time-no one is entirely responsible for your failure. You can change the direction of your life. Recalibrate the GPS of your life today. Now is the time for a change. Revolution starts in the mind. Stick to the desired pattern of thoughts. Focus on those thoughts relentlessly. We follow the path of our dominant thought. We create dominant thoughts by repetition. Roll those thoughts over and over again. John Locke said "reading furnishes the mind only with materials of knowledge; it is thinking that makes what we read ours". Meditate on the word. We grow and develop by degrees from the word of God. Meditation on the word bears all our progression.

Joshua 1:8 (This book of the law shall not depart out of thy mouth; but thou shalt meditate therein day and night, that thou mayest observe to do according to all that is written therein: for then thou shalt make thy way prosperous, and then thou shalt have good success.)

Success is predictable because all your daily habits contribute like compounded interest towards your tomorrow. You can make your way prosperous by meditation on proper things. Muse on the word, consider it thoughtfully. Mutter on the word, speak it under your breath. Meditating on the word means to reflect, contemplate, plan and regurgitate. Furnish your mind with the whole counsel of God. A consistent mental picture will eventually develop and manifest. Meditation on the word rewires your mind in accordance with God's will. Meditation makes you realize God's promises.

Acquire skills and knowledge that will assist you in improving and taking your life to the next level. Be a good teacher and learner at the same time. I did not know that I could work twenty hours a day until I had to do it. I didn't know that I could push an inoperable vehicle to the side of the road alone until I had to do it. We can stretch when life calls for it. There is latent potential in you.

There is a need for us to stretch. Athletes, soccer players, and various sportsmen exercise in order to stretch. It is amazing to find out how much you can do when subjected to a certain pressure of the situation. A difference between graphite and diamonds is the pressure that was applied and exerted to them, they all have a common base of carbon. Much of who we are cannot come out due to the lack of pressure. Many people want to be diamonds but dislike the cutting process. Take an extra shot at everything that you do. Psychologists say that we use about 10% of our brains and 90% lies idle without being utilized at all-untapped capacity. There is a lot of untapped strength, ability, potential, capability, and treasure. Your mind is a vault packed with treasure. Scientists say that there is enough atomic power in a slice of bread to power an ocean-liner but the challenge is for us to extract that power. The atoms in the bread are more stable and difficult to separate but the ones in uranium are unstable and we tend to use them. Release what is in you.

When something is not used for a long time it begins to be rusty and it depreciates in value. Stretch until you become what God has called you to be. Do not die just as you are but as purposed by God. You will not become different by doing the same old things that you are doing. Change what you are doing and you will be different. What you do today has a cumulative effect on what you will be tomorrow.

If a farmer wants to change a harvest, he will change the seeds because a seed determines the kind of harvest. A seed is programmed with inherent and specific details of what it is and what it should become. A seed has a specific nature and instructions and when placed in the ground it only begins to manifest the contents in it due to the pressure and other various conducive elements that create an appropriate atmosphere. A seed will never bear a forest when it is placed on a dining table-it needs proper surroundings and conditions. We need to get away from our comfort zones and be courageous to be what God has called us to be. The comfort zone is characterized by unfruitfulness, unprofitability, wastage, un-resourcefulness, disorder, contraction and procrastination. Stretching brings more strength, better shape, versatility, flexibility, dexterity and durability. Paul stretched himself until he said, 'I have finished my course, I have kept the faith, and I have run the race'. The finishing, keeping, and running, all require discipline and stretching. Stretch and become an asset and not a liability.

It's time for expansion. Desire to increase and enlarge. You have stayed in one condition for too long. You have over-stayed your welcome. Your parking ticket has expired, you need to move. You have outgrown that place, you are uncomfortable. God is leading you out of that place. Engage in some writing, this helps to expand your mind. Have a diary where you write what would have happened daily. Practice some drawing. Rub your shoulders with thinkers. Successful people don't waste time watching television programming that does not help them in advancing. Our minds should not be under-developed, under-utilized, under-explored and under-invested.

It is estimated that 60 % of all jobs in the USA today require some type of college degree. Ignorance restricts and hinders your growth fundamentally. The difference between success and failure is in information. In a knowledge-based economy, you earn what you learn. Learning is a cornerstone to development and growth. No man has a monopoly on wisdom, so actively pursue some. Pursuit is the proof of desire. Thinking like peasants will close doors to palaces. Before you write, think. Make it a concrete resolution to acquire information. 90% of new-year resolutions fail and 30% of them are breached within the first month.

People are destroyed for lack of knowledge of the word, where God reveals his will. Rejecting knowledge causes us to be rejected and forgotten by God as seen in Hosea 4v6. Lack of knowledge is working against your destiny. Ignorance is fatal.

Ignorance is an enabler for pride, supports fear, and will throw you off target. It can cripple your progress, causing accidents and incidents that could delay, bind and limit you, bringing denials to your life. Ignorance:

- devalues you
- releases generational backwardness
- crashes you
- defuses you
- truncates opportunities
- drowns you
- increases risk
- cuts your return on investment
- lengthens trouble
- causes complaining
- robs you
- wastes time
- fights virtue
- creates vagueness
- brings settlement for less
- advocates for an average life
- derails assignment
- encourages pettiness
- accentuates poverty
- brings dependence
- creates excuses
- demeans you
- demotes you
- short-circuits your goals
- deports you from the elite status

CHAPTER THREE

A NEW MIND

"If you never change your mind, why have one?" Edward de Bono

Luke 5:37-38 'And no man putteth new wine into old bottles; else the new wine will burst the bottles, and be spilled, and the bottles shall perish. But new wine must be put into new bottles; and both are preserved.'

Jesus uses this story to explain critical points about the mind. Putting new wine into old wineskins will compromise both-the wine will be lost and the wineskins will burst. New wine needs new wineskins or bottles. God cannot do the new with the old mind. The old mind will lose opportunities, time and can't seize the present. The old mind will suffocate the flow of heavenly abundance in our lives. When wine is fermenting it goes through changes that the old wineskins cannot accommodate. In the Hebraic culture, old wineskins have to be put in water and then in oil latter for them to be renewed. The water represents the word and the oil stands for the holy-ghost. We need the water and the oil for the renewal of our minds. A new mind will not incubate or sit upon wrong thoughts until they hatch. We are commanded to be transformed by the renewal of our minds. Conformity eradicates our uniqueness and distinction. A new mind does not compromise with sin.

"Isaiah 43:19 *"Behold, I will do a new thing; now it shall spring forth; shall ye not know it? I will even make a way in the wilderness, and rivers in the desert."*

A new day without a new mind is not meaningful. An old mind will leak opportunities and blessings. The new mind will maximize on the new wine. Decide to be blessed, to be happy, to be peaceful and to rejoice,

Psalms 118:26 "This is the day which the LORD hath made; we will rejoice and be glad in it."

What you think about yourself will determine other people's reaction towards you. Your image formed and forged by your thoughts will speak for you. The word of God which is forever settled in heaven should be settled in your mind, heart and mouth. Then it will manifest.

For decades, a building can sit abandoned and deteriorating. The old landmark can be in danger of degrading past the point of restoration by the time developers step in and begin the transformation of the old structure. But there is hope because renovation can bring this old building into its new state again.

The prefix 're' in the words renovate, refresh, restore and renew means 'again'. The old building doesn't have to be destroyed, it should just be renewed. The same goes for our minds. We don't have to cut our heads off but just to renew them with the word of God. If we don't change what we know, we can't change our beliefs. We need the renewal. A new mind is a clear mind, free from haze and mist-it's needed for accomplishing much in life. A cluttered, confused and disordered state of the mind clogs the flow in our lives. It offers friction to the movement of ideas and thoughts. We are commanded to have the mind of Christ. Christ is the word. Therefore, we have the mind of the word. The word has to become our dominant thought.

The word brings renewal, renovation, repair and restoration to our minds. God restores our souls.

John 17:17 (Sanctify them through thy truth: thy word is truth)

Water covers 70 % of the Earth's surface and is vital for all known forms of life. About 96 % of the planet's water is found in oceans. In physiology, body water is the water content of the human body. About 60 % of our bodies is water. Safe drinking water is essential to humans and other life forms even though it provides no calories or organic nutrients. About one billion people still lack access to safe water. Water is tasteless and odorless. We can't live without water. The word of God is represented by water. The word gives us life just like water does to the physical life. The word washes us thoroughly. The word of God removes all complexes, fears, toxins and negativities from us. We cannot live without the word. We desperately need it. If your mind is not transformed you could be saved but still walk in the same problems you walked in before you were saved. When you allow outside negative thoughts to get inside, then you begin to sink. Either you sink or get rid of those unproductive thoughts.

Your opportunities are not in the realm of the comfortable but well beyond that. There are places you need to go and an un-renewed mind is keeping you back. Continue to occupy your space and possessions. Perception can block your opportunities. Some invest during an economic depression and become millionaires. Others stand aloof and miss the rich opportunities. The renewed mind is a carousel of progress because it maximizes the moment by seizing opportunities.

The word transformation is used three times in the bible. One of the times it is used is in the transfiguration of Jesus Christ. Transformation means transfiguration. Transfiguration means a change in form and appearance. We are transfigured and transformed by the renewing of our minds. Renewing our minds brings the change we desire and need over a process. We cannot shift in life till we shift in the mind. Developmental change in our lives is derived from a renewed mind. It takes time for a tadpole to turn into a frog. It's a process for a silk worm to turn into a butterfly. It takes time for diamonds to be made through extreme and high pressure from carbon rich materials. Move your mind into a more acceptable position or state by the word of God. Just like the salmon is diadromous, meaning that it changes from a freshwater to a saltwater lifestyle-we are to change from one position of thinking to another. The level of thinking can shift the level of life.

When we are born again, our spirits are completely made anew. Our souls are being saved and our bodies shall ultimately be saved. We should renew our minds daily. We should not be pressured into the matrix, frame or model of the systems of the world. Conforming to the world happens from the outside and going in. We are not to comply and be in harmony with the world. Agreeing and giving the same shape and contour as the world will pull us away from living in God's will. The renewal of our minds is the work of the Holy Spirit and the word of God. The Holy Spirit uses the word that you would have taken in to renovate your mind. We can be enemies of God and alienated from Him in our minds as seen in Colossians 1:21. God keeps us in perfect peace when our minds are stayed on him. Our minds should continue to be in a place or condition of being inclined on God. We have to spend time, continue, sojourn and remain fixed on God.

We need to shift our thinking from one way to another-a fundamental change in approach and direction. The way of doing things need to change. The internet, which is a network of networks has literally brought a shift to our way of doing things-we now pay bills, we order clothes, go to school, find a job, read the news, watch movies, communicate with each other, banking, investing, playing games, chatting, surfing, listening to music and many more online. The internet makes it possible for millions of people to share knowledge in the minutest of time. Indeed, we live in a global village.

We are all connected through the internet. It has brought access to all forms of content. In the same vein, the shift in our thinking shifts the way of doing things. The way of doing things shifts our future.

Summary Points
- *New wine needs new wineskins*
- *Old mindset can't accommodate the new*
- *The word has to become our dominant thought*
- *Developmental change comes from a renewed mind*
- *The shift in our thinking will shift our mode of operation*

CHAPTER FOUR

STRONGHOLDS OF THE MIND

"Christianity is the greatest intellectual system the mind of man has ever touched."
Francis Schaeffer

2 Corinthians 10:4 (For the weapons of our warfare are not carnal, but mighty through God to the pulling down of strong holds)

Science has found out that a human being is also wired for spiritual experiences, this new study is called Neuro-theology. But those spiritual experiences are the reason for battle. We are in a war but that war is in the mind. There are weapons that we should use to fight imaginations, pictures and thoughts which are not of God. The devil works his way into our lives through our minds. Strange, evil and wicked thoughts are injected by the enemy. Immerse your mind in the word of God. Jesus was crucified in a place named Golgotha, which means "Place of a Skull", to defeat all wars and battles of the mind. The skull is a case that encloses and protects the chief sense organs and supports the jaws. The skull is a protective vault. His head was crowned with thorns. Thorns represent curses that attack our minds but Jesus overcame them. He said, "it is finished". He dealt with all thoughts from the devil that are meant to torment us. Strongholds represent a captured area that has been fortified by the enemy. These are areas of our minds that have been surrendered over to the devil. Also, a stronghold is a strong group of thoughts. It is a place of survival or refuge, an area dominated or occupied by the enemy. The devil brings fear, darkness to your mind. He blurs and blinds your mind. Fear is honoring the words of men more than the words of God. We need to dethrone the enemy and possess our minds. Remove the chains that bind you in Jesus name.

James 4:7 (Submit yourselves therefore to God. Resist the devil, and he will flee from you).

Resist the ideas that the devil throws in your mind. The devil is known by many names and one of them is the Greek word "diabolos" which means one prone to slander, accusing falsely, a calumniator, false accuser, slanderer, or one who throws ideas. Adam and Eve succumbed to the ideas of the devil and they ate the forbidden fruit. The ideas to Eve and Adam were attractive. Jesus experienced the same attack from the devil, but he resisted by the word as shown in *Mathew 4:4 (But he answered and said, It is written, Man shall not live by bread alone, but by every word that proceedeth out of the mouth of God.).* Devil's ideas can be resisted by God's ideas. That's the law of displacement.

Possessing your mind is the secret to possessing other things in life. The devil twisted the word as he approached Adam and Eve. He managed to twist their minds and their lives were twisted. Subsequently history has been twisted ever since. But the devil could not twist Jesus's mind. Jesus won the battles and wars of the mind on our behalf. The law enforcement agencies across the USA, using automated scanners, have gathered millions of digital records on the location and movement of every vehicle with a license plate, according to studies done recently. These scanners are fastened to police cars, bridges or buildings, they capture images of passing or parked vehicles and note their location, uploading and transferring that information into police databases. Departments keep the records for weeks or years, sometimes indefinitely. In the same vein we need to scan all thoughts that go into our minds and oust every thought that is against the will of God. You can't be naïve to entertain every thought to your detriment, loss and harm. We need to know the state of our minds. We are stewards and custodians of our minds. We need to take ownership or else our minds will lead us astray. It's easier to destroy a thought in its embryonic stage than latter when it's built into a stronghold.

We have the ability to pull down strongholds in our minds. By the time you are 20 years old, you would have seen about 50,000 beer commercials and about 40,000 murders on the television, internet, magazines and billboards. Advertising is a $250 billion/year industry. If you hear the word of God for 30 minutes every Sunday for one year, that's about 26 hours. 26 hours is about one full day. One full day per year cannot change years of negative thinking and programming in your mind. We need an overdose of the word. Be word-minded for you to win the battle of the mind. Set your mind on things that are above and not on those that are beneath. Settle it in your mind that you are sound and your life will follow suit. We are commanded to have the mind of Christ and the life of Christ will follow. If your mind is not prospering, your life will not prosper. We are living at the degree of our thinking. We are to gird the loins of our mind or else we will become like chameleons that take on colors from our surroundings. We are driven by our thoughts but we can control and choose our thoughts. There is an adage that says "You can't keep the birds from flying over your head, but you can keep them from building nests in your hair." Pull down all imaginations that are against God's will. Imaginations are a formation of mental images. Television programming is rendering images to our minds and we need to be selective of our ingestion and consumption.

Psalm 66:12 "Thou hast caused men to ride over our heads; we went through fire and through water: but thou broughtest us out into a wealthy place."

War chariots were sent to crush the skulls of Israel in slavery. They traveled through fire and through floods, but God brought them to a land of plenty and abundance. The devil is after our heads. Psalm 3:3 says that "But thou, O Lord, art a shield for me; my glory, and the lifter up of mine head". The devil is after our heads because our heads are in charge and in leadership of the design of our lives. In 1 Samuel 17:51, we see that David ran over and pulled out Goliath's sword. Then he used it to cut off Goliath's head. When the Philistines saw what had happened to their hero, they started running away. David cut the head of Goliath and the enemies army was scattered. Psalm 23:5 shows us that God prepares a table for us in the presence of our enemies. He anoints our heads with oil and our brimming cups run over. Ecclesiastes 2:14 depicts that a wise man's eyes are in his head, but the fool walks in darkness; and yet in the end one event happens to them both. One event happens to them both but those with eyes will see and perceive it. The battles that you overcome in the mind are portals for your promotion.

Summary Points
- *A twisted mind births a twisted life.*
- *We are custodians of our minds.*
- *Strongholds are areas in our mind captured by the devil.*
- *Be word-minded to win the battle of your mind.*
- *The battles you overcome become the portal to your promotion.*

CHAPTER FIVE

THE LIMITED MIND

"God created the world; the laws of nature were created by God. True science tries to find out what God put in the world. The trouble is where scientists speculate about theology and they don't know what they're talking about because they weren't there. They can't speculate about the origins of life because they weren't there." *Pat Robertson*

"There are no great limits to growth because there are no limits of human intelligence, imagination, and wonder" *Ronald Reagan*

Psalm 78:41 (Yea, they turned back and tempted God, and limited the Holy One of Israel).

God is not limited. God said to Abraham that he was his exceeding reward and shield as noted in Genesis 15:1. Abraham was told to go out of the tent to observe and count the stars. God was expanding his mind and removing limits from it. The stars are innumerable. God has a blessing that no room can contain. Abraham's vision from God was far-fetched and large. His mind was supposed to accommodate the dream. Abraham was childless and old. His wife was old too but God isn't limited by time, matter or anything. There are limitless opportunities to the unlimited mind. The limit on the mind determine the size of our world. The limited mind creates a limited life. Don't deal with the limits on the outside only but with those on the inside and the rest will change. A shrinking mind is satiated by little and minute achievements. There is more for the taking. Don't be the richest man in the graveyard due to dying with untapped potential.

Judges 6:12 (And the angel of the LORD appeared unto him, and said unto him, The LORD is with thee, thou mighty man of velour)

See yourself as God sees you. God will use you if you see yourself as he sees you. Gideon saw himself as the least, the last and the lost. He looked at his weaknesses, instead of God's strength. He lectured God about his frailties and how he couldn't do nothing. God can do the impossible through us but we need to change our retrogressive dominant thoughts. Gideon's best thinking had brought him to this position of unbelief. Gideon wasn't unwrapping the infinite greatness in him, he miniaturized it. You are entitled to your thinking and every thought is permissible but not every thought is beneficial. Gideon was in a conflict between the message he was hearing from the angel and the message in his mind. This conflict brings chaos, confusion and disorder. Gideon had excuses and was not confident. Gideon resorted to the default or the comfort zone of his mind instead of interrupting it by God's message. He had to entertain the interruption in order to change. Some believe in others only and not in themselves. Gideon's success was predicated on him reversing the negative beliefs and believing in God. Don't deny that something is wrong. You can't fix what you can't confront. What you allow and permit, you can't change.

Gideon had to go past his history and create a new story. He had to come to a point of closure with his past and experiences. Dismiss what pulls you back. Get over past mistakes. Failure is not final. Holding onto past mistakes is working backwards. Inferiority was tattooed in Gideon's mind. Don't put limits on yourself. Gideon had to overcome some blind spots. About 80 members of the Stanford

School of Business Council were asked to recommend the most vital capability of the successful. Unanimously they gave one answer, that is, "to know who you are". Gideon didn't know who he was. Take time to know who you are in God.

Gideon never saw that he was valiant. Our lives reflect on our thought processes. Also, others relate to us based on the reflection of our thoughts about them. David did not accept the armor from Saul. He used his sling and stones because he had faith in what he had. You have what it takes to defeat your enemies and foes. Failure is based on wrong thinking. We need to be delivered from the clutches of mental oppression and bondage. Relive moments and times of joy. Don't rehearse the bad times. Shake off the condemnation. You can't change your past-keep moving and make better choices. Don't allow that clutter in your mind, it makes you unhappy.

Joshua 14:10 (And now, behold, the LORD hath kept me alive, as he said, these forty and five years, even since the LORD spake this word unto Moses, while the children of Israel wandered in the wilderness: and now, lo, I am this day fourscore and five years old.)

When Caleb son of Jephunneh the Kenizzite was forty years old, he was sent by Moses the servant of the Lord from Kadesh-barnea to scout out the promise land. Caleb and Joshua brought to Moses a good report. But the other ten brethren made the hearts of the people of Israel to melt because they brought an evil report. Yet Caleb and Joshua wholly followed the Lord God. On that day Moses swore that Caleb and his children would inherit the land, because he wholly followed the Lord God. And at eighty-five years old, Caleb came to ask for his inheritance. Caleb asked for a new challenge at eighty-five years of age. Caleb knew that he was not too old to set another goal or to dream again. What we accomplish in life is small as compared to what we could do-the possibilities are limitless. Take action on a daily basis towards your vision. Manifestations are congruent to the degree of your belief. You have the power to change. Your level of commitment determines the level of your returns from your dream. On a daily basis, do things and read materials that empower and invigorate you. Go up in life because you are not wired to be the least.

If you don't program yourself, you will be programmed by your surroundings-you can't live in a vacuum. When the fear is greater than the realization of your dreams, your dreams will fail. You must remain focused on your process to your promise and provision. The way you perceive life has a lot to do with how far you can go. Life is made out of great possibilities, but they can be eradicated by small thinking. Never doubt the greatness that God has placed in you. Great things happen when you sacrifice-be willing to drop some things along the way. Don't allow circumstances to control you, they are just a process-don't be stuck in the process-destiny is calling you. Greatness is waiting for you. Work through the mental blocks. Stretching can show you more of what you didn't know you could do.

A limited mind does not entertain details. It just dwells on the surface. Limited minds miss opportunities. We should not be narrow and restricted. More strength and force are gained by moving from a limited life into an unlimited one. Remove enclosing and confining barriers. Be intense, ardent and driven by what you do. Take advantage of all situations including adversity. Apply your mind to your mission. Limited minds see a life without options and possibilities. Try seeing life through all dimensions. A mind in a closet will produce limited results-come out of it. The mind is so expanse and was not designed to shrink, do more with it. It is of great extent and can spread out. It takes negative energy to reduce yourself to limited borders. We were created to dominate the earth. The word 'dominate' has same roots as the word 'kingdom'. We have a domain or a territory over which authority is exercised. We are royal. We can limit the domain by our thoughts. It's all at our disposal for the taking. A reaction is an idea evoked by some experience. We are either reactive or proactive in life. Being proactive is the tendency to initiate change. Unlimited minds are proactive.

When the prodigal son was returning to his father, he had made up his mind to be a slave. But when he got back to his dad, he was received as a son. The father wants us to have the mind of sons and not slaves. Slaves don't own anything but sons have rights and inheritance. He limited his thinking by the things he went through. He allowed his temporary experiences to define him. His experiences demoted him from son-ship. Don't go down to the level of your mistakes. We are held back by our ignorance. In this world we hear more of our limitations than our potentials.

Many great actors did not take any acting courses or degrees but are very successful, having accolades and trophies for outstanding works. They tapped into a God-given talent and gift. Education is important but being educated in a God-given area is more profitable. They did not limit themselves due to the lack of a certificate. But had a mindset to excel in their potential and purpose. Don't disqualify yourself. Today the average CEO is about 30 years-no more limitations in terms of age or gender. Stir up the gifts in you. Make vital decisions within the parameters of your purpose. Many are the plans of men but God's purpose prevails.

Coercive persuasion, mind abuse, menticide, thought control, or thought reform, all these refer to a process in which an individual deliberately and systematically uses unethically manipulative methods to persuade others to conform to the wishes of the manipulator. The devil desires to limit us by persuading us to believe his lies. He is the father of all lies and if we are not careful, we can believe a lie for the rest of our lives. Whose report are we believing? God's report leads to abundance. The devil's report leads to destruction and loss. Don't believe his accusations. We are made in God's image and likeness. We are victors and not victims. We are not limited by the enemy. We are under an open heaven that showers blessings in our lives.

No more limits. We break limits. Think big. Someone's limited and twisted opinion of you should not become your reality.

Summary Points
- *The limit on your mind determines the limit on your world*
- *You can't fix what you can't confront*
- *Failure is based on wrong thinking*
- *Don't define yourself by a temporary event*
- *Unlimited minds are proactive*

CHAPTER SIX

THE VISIONARY'S MIND

"Minds are like parachutes; they only function when open" (Thomas Dewer)

Proverbs 29:18 (Where there is no vision, the people perish: but he that keepeth the law, happy is he.)

Mark Cuban had the habit of looking at big, expensive and beautiful houses, and he would provoke himself to work creatively so as to reach a level of affording them. That dream and passion catapulted him to billionaire status. The mind is such a powerful asset and it has the ability to transform words into pictures. This is why you are able to visualize a person just by hearing them on the radio. You might not come up with the exact picture but the information in your mind makes one anywhere. It is tragic to see and not have vision. If you are casual about your dream, you become a casualty.

Ephesians 3:20 (Now all glory to God, who is able, through his mighty power at work within us, to accomplish infinitely more than we might ask or think)

This bible verse talks about God giving us above what we ask nor think but the question is what are you thinking? The very thing you are thinking about will be used by God for his multiplication. If you are thinking nothing, then nothing will be multiplied and the product is zero. If you are thinking little then that is the only medium for multiplication. Your thoughts are the multiplication factor that God uses. The word of God is the mind of God and should be induced into our minds. We find our visions in the word of God. To be carnally minded is death, this shows that the mind has a direct relationship to our destiny-death or life. Carnal thinking leads to death. Death speaks of separation between God and man. Our thinking separates us from God. The prodigal son separated himself from his father and connected himself to pigs. He left the father's system of provision and attached himself to the world's system of provision.

As we go to the word we should get it and think on it until we become as it says, that is meditation (Joshua 1:8). Meditation on the word brings success and prosperity. Affect your thinking process and patterns by the word. Take time to meditate on a daily basis. Meditation makes you to take the word to the sub-conscious mind and every function from the sub-conscious mind is involuntary. You do not have to think for your heart to beat because that is an involuntary action. Doing good will become involuntary when you hide God's word in you. Your predominant thoughts will control the path of your life. A clean mind will permit the control of the Holy Spirit over your life. Today's thoughts are powerful seeds for tomorrow's actions. The visionary who has an impoverished mindset will not prosper due to limitations. The poverty mentality will always find substitutes for God. A. W. Tozer said that 'what comes to our mind when we think of God-is the most important part of us'.

All winners in life are big dreamers. You are greatly awarded for your vision and not just for your work. You might not have the money for the project but the vision will attract the provision. A dream is a seed of greatness. A dream has power to influence and affect the world. Warren G. Bennis said that "leadership is the capacity to translate vision into reality". The genius and creativity of world-class organizations is embedded in their visions. A narrow vision will produce small results. Don't see things as they are but as they ought to be, that's the essence of seeing into the future. Your voice, fingerprints, and eyes are absolutely unique and specific to you. Out of the seven billion people in the whole world, you are the only one with that particular assignment. Don't limit your assignment to the size of your financial account.

Between your dream and its manifestation, there are odds and adversities that you should overcome. God will bring to completion what he has started in you-that dream will not die. Vision affects the way you perceive situations, there is a hope that is injected in you. A restricted vision will strangle the possibilities of realities. Visions pull and stretch us to higher places and altitudes. Where there is a vision, things begin to fall in place inadvertently. We synthesize, think and exert our energies within the parameters of the vision. The vision creates our field of influence. Strength is a vital part in the execution of the vision. Do something with the dream which God has given you. Scarcity of vision is scarcity of production and results. A strategic vision shows us where we are going in a clear fashion. Vision doesn't just consist of mere speech but strategic activity, logical thinking and work. Don't build your vision around the negatives of the past. Vision is connected to prosperity, advancement and achievement.

It takes one man with an idea and a vision to change the world. Ray Kroc had a creative vision of a hamburger and some fries. He worked on this vision tenaciously. Today the McDonald's Corporation is the world's largest chain of hamburger fast food restaurants, serving around 68 million customers daily in 119 countries. McDonald's revenue for the year 2012 was 6.9 billion. Ray was true to his vision.

His perceptive dreams were unlimited and they are still speaking even after his death. Ray was an idea-preneur, who generated new and innovative ideas. A business or nation without a vision will go through economic recessionary times.

Every city has the feel and the texture of the vision of the mayor of that city. All organizations rise and fall on the back of the visionary. People are suffering in an area that you are not serving them with your dream. This dream can only be done by you. Never push your dreams into the future, begin to work on them now. Don't kill your dream by promoting your limitations. You deserve more than you are having, or doing, or seeing right now. True vision outlasts the visionary. It lives even after his death. Your dream is possible. Remove strength drainers-they suck out your energy and passion.

Summary Points
- *Vision attracts provision*
- *Don't kill your dream by promoting your limitations*
- *Maximize the spectrum of your mindset and inevitably the latitude of your production will be maximized*
- *Don't see yourself for who you are but for who you could be*
- *Don't complain about the fear you permit*

CHAPTER SEVEN

A TRANSFORMED MIND

"The Bible is a revelation of the mind and will of God to men. Therein we may learn, what God is" Jupiter Hammon

Romans 12:1-2: "I beseech you therefore, brethren, by the mercies of God, that ye present your bodies a living sacrifice, holy, acceptable unto God, which is your reasonable service. And be not conformed to this world: but be ye transformed by the renewing of your mind, that ye may prove what is that good, and acceptable, and perfect, will of God."

Paul urges us not to be patterned after the design of this world. We should not comply to the standards of the world but the word. Don't use the methods of the world. Method is the manner of procedure, especially a regular and systematic way of accomplishing something. Don't shape yourself according to the vain stimuli of the world. Shape your life around the positives and not the negatives. The word 'transform' comes from a word that means metamorphosis. Metamorphosis is an alteration in nature that takes a process. It is a long and arduous process. It requires strenuous exercise. Metamorphosis entails exertion and pressure. One person said that "ideas that enter the mind under fire remain there securely and forever". The world can shape you if you let it. When the word alters your mind, your lifestyle is altered too. The thought-forms have to be made around the word. Transform the way you think about yourself. Don't wait until a crisis happens for you to change. When we renew our minds, we are transformed, and we can prove his will-the good, acceptable and perfect will of God. The renewal of the mind is linked and connected to the will of God. We can hinder or allow God's will by our mindset. The degree to which you can prove the will of God is predicated on the mind. Renewal brings a change in appearance, character, condition and function of the mind. Don't conform to the pattern of this world. The Greek word for world is "kosmos", which means systems. These systems are great but have been corrupted and defiled by the unspiritual men. These systems run by faithful men will produce high yields. In the banking system we can cite, predatory lending. This is the unfair, deceptive, or fraudulent practices of some lenders during the loan origination process.

The terrible Global financial crisis of 2008, is considered by many economic experts to have been the worst financial crisis since the Great Depression of the 1930s. It threatened the eminent collapse of big financial institutions, which was prevented by the bailout of banks by governments, but stock markets still dropped worldwide. The housing market also suffered, resulting in evictions, foreclosures and prolonged unemployment.

Some of the systems that require faithful leadership.
- *Welfare*
- *Banking*
- *Financial*
- *Healthcare*
- *Educational*
- *Political*
- *Business*
- *Mortgage*
- *Marketing*

- *Accounting*
- *Commerce*
- *Security*
- *Media*
- *Medical*

Broadcast media such as radio, recorded music, film and television transmit their information electronically to large audiences. Print media use a physical object such as a newspaper, book, pamphlet or comics, to distribute their information. Outdoor media is a form of mass media that comprises billboards, signs or placards placed inside and outside of commercial buildings, sports stadiums, shops and buses. Internet media provides many mass media services, such as email, websites, blogs, and internet based radio and television. The media is a suffocating swirl that affects our thinking but we should not be squeezed into its negative mold. We should not adopt the worldly way of doing things. Transformation is inward.

Summary Points
- *Transformation means transfiguration*
- *Transformation is a change of form*
- *We are transformers and not conformers*
- *Renewal brings transformation*
- *Repentance is a change of mind*
- *Transformation or metamorphosis is a long process*
- *Degree of renewal is the degree of change*
- *We present our bodies through a renewed mind*
- *The will of God is realized through a renewed mind*
- *Renewal comes by the word of God*
- *A renewed mind breaks oppressive systems*

CHAPTER EIGHT

IMAGINATIONS OF THE MIND

"Your world is a living expression of how you are using and have used your mind."
Earl Nightingale

The mind was created for memory and imagination. David said to Saul "Your Majesty, I take care of my father's sheep. And when one of them is dragged off by a lion or a bear, I go after it and beat the wild animal until it lets the sheep go. If the wild animal turns and attacks me, I grab it by the throat and kill it. Sir, I have killed lions and bears that way, and I can kill this worthless Philistine. He shouldn't have made fun of the army of the living God! The LORD has rescued me from the claws of lions and bears, and he will keep me safe from the hands of this Philistine." When David talked of the lions and the bears, he was using his memory. When he talked of killing the worthless Goliath, he was using his imagination. See that Goliath falling down in your imagination. Every battle is primarily won in the territory of your mind and then what happens outside is only secondary. Hit a homerun in your mind first.

Lamentations 3:60: (Thou hast seen all their vengeance and all their imaginations against me.)

Earl D. Radmacher said "you are capable of recording 800 memories per second for 75 years without ever getting tired. The mind is a powerful tool. God has given us the power to imagine. Playing is learning for children, usually they laugh and joke with imaginary friends. This is good for their imaginations. The mind can travel to places you have never been through the power of imagination. The mind can go to places that the body is too tired to get to. The mind should not be used for memory alone but also for imagination. Imagination is the ability to form new images and sensations. Imagination can evoke new worlds. Albert Einstein said, "Imagination ... is more important than knowledge. Knowledge is limited. Imagination encircles the world." The imagination goes beyond sight, hearing, tasting and smelling. Thank God for imagination because with it we can see beyond the present problems and circumstances.

We all have images of ourselves, our families, our future and so forth within our minds but what kind of images are they? Have an image of all the promises of God and they will come to pass in your life. It's God's way to use pictures in transferring a vision to us. If you can see it, God will do it. Many cancer patients live much better before they know that they have cancer. The announcement of cancer creates an image of sickness and death. This negative image begins to develop within them to their detriment. Today we have television programing that is aiding our minds with negative images. Your mind can go back in the past and collect horrible pictures and stuff or it can go into the future and see the bright horizons.

2 Corinthians 10v5: (Casting down imaginations, and every high thing that exalteth itself against the knowledge of God and bringing into captivity every thought to the obedience of Christ;).

The devil is very subtle and he dresses himself up as an angel of light. He steals, kills and destroys silently. We are engaged in a long and protracted war with the devil. And the battleground is the mind.

We are to pull down imaginations that are against Christ. The devil fights us in the mind. We are to cast down imaginations and every high thing that exalts itself against the knowledge of Christ. All thoughts should pay obeisance to Christ. Any rebellious thought to Christ should be expelled. Pull down the nation of negative images in you.

What the mind can do is incalculable. An artist never finishes his work because the options and possibilities are just too wide and very deep. The best of buildings was once an image in the mind before it was imposed on paper and eventually built. The international organization Council on Tall Buildings currently ranks Burj Khalifa as the tallest at (2,717 ft). This building is in Dubai, United Arab Emirates. Construction began on 21 September 2004, with the exterior of the structure completed on 1 October 2009. It took 6 years to translate an image born in the mind to fruition. There is a lot in our minds. There are poems, songs, dance styles, stories, books, inventions latent in us and should not go to the grave. You carry more than you can imagine. We produce what we invoke in our minds through passion and repetition. You can't produce that which is inconsistent with your thinking. Thinking imaginatively is a part of creativity. We live in a busy world-the hustle and bustle can hinder imaginations. Also due to the technological age, we have outsourced our minds to the computer. But our potential is limitless.

At age 66, Colonel Sanders lost his business and began to live on his Social security check. But he worked his way up to become a multimillionaire. Even at an advanced age he imagined the impossible. Your mind is a creative tool. Activate inspiration and intuition by for example, taking a walk and writing some thoughts. Start using a journal, you never know when your eureka moment will stumble on you. Also write down all your ideas, notes and to-do lists. Remember to think on paper. Pictures can be carved in the mind. Pictures carved in the mind become a reality. Be a sculptor of the right pictures.

History has it that the Wright brothers, Orville and Wilbur were two American brothers, inventors, and aviation pioneers who were credited with inventing and building the world's first successful airplane and making the first controlled, powered and sustained heavier-than-air human flight, on December 17, 1903. In 1878 their dad, who traveled often as a bishop in the Church of the United Brethren in Christ, brought home a toy "helicopter" for his two sons. Made of paper, bamboo and cork with a rubber band to twirl its rotor, it was about a foot long. Wilbur and Orville played with it until it broke, and then built their own. In later years, they pointed to their experience with the toy as the initial spark of their interest in flying-it ignited their imagination.

Summary points.
- *Change the latitude, longitude and space of your mind and your world will follow suit.*
- *Don't be the richest in the grave.*
- *A negative mindset will not produce a positive lifestyle.*
- *Kill the settlement mentality.*
- *Aim for excellence and not perfection.*

CHAPTER NINE

THE NEGATIVE MIND

Positive thinking will let you do everything better than negative thinking will.
Zig Ziglar

"There is an attitude of faith that makes it possible to live in the midst of trouble without being troubled." — Jerry Savelle

Acts 14:2: (But the unbelieving Jews stirred up the Gentiles, and made their minds evil affected against the brethren.)

The above portion of scripture depicts that, they made their minds evil. Have you ever wondered how a mind can keep an event that happened 30 years ago so fresh?. Many people say, "It's like it happened yesterday". When events happen in a traumatic way they leave an indelible mark on us and hence it is not easy to forget them. Also rehearsing the thought will keep it updated. You should maintain an atmosphere of creativity by getting rid of damaging and negative thoughts. The battle is between the two ears. The mind can have worse pictures than those that can be portrayed in a Hollywood movie. A wounded and maimed mind like a body can suffer great pain. Your pain alters your perception of the world and others at large. A damaged and broken life will not allow you to enjoy the high moment. Don't think from a shame-based identity. Just like the body, your mind is designed to heal. Godly music and the word of God heal the mind. The mind determines your view of life.

Psalms 23v3: (He restoreth my soul: he leadeth me in the paths of righteousness for his name's sake).

David confesses that the Lord restores his mind. I took an old sofa that was broken down for upholstery and through the craftsman's expertise he managed to restore it to its original state. Our minds can be restored. Automobile restoration is the process of fixing the lower quality of an automobile to revert it to its original intended condition. It is to refurbish a car and keep in line with how it would have looked when first presented for sale. Our minds can be restored. A restored vehicle can be more expensive than a non-restored one. When God restores your mind, your intrinsic sense of value increases.

Genesis 2v19: (*And out of the ground the* LORD *God formed every beast of the field, and every fowl of the air; and brought them unto Adam to see what he would call them: and whatsoever Adam called every living creature, that was the name thereof*).

God brought all the animals to Adam. Whatever he called them was final. God had no objection. That's a brilliant mind. The bird's category alone has thousands of species. So Adam was busy in the garden. But when he sinned he lost the glory and the mind has never been the same. Sin degraded the level of thinking. But Jesus came to restore us hence when he was on the cross, they put a crown of thorns on him. The crown represented restoration to our minds. We now have the mind of Christ as seen in *1 Corinthians 2v16: (For who hath known the mind of the Lord, that he may instruct him? but we have the mind of Christ).*

Your emotions and thoughts should not be manipulated and controlled by a trauma or events that happened in your life.

Manipulation, intimidation, condemnation and control define witchcraft. Don't be bewitched by thoughts of the past. Don't be haunted by the past. Other people's evil choices should not imprison you. Don't allow external conditions to affect internal choices. When the devil reminds you of your past-remind him of his future. The devil's future is the lake of fire. Your future is so bright and full of bliss.

Exodus 1v13: (And the Egyptians made the children of Israel to serve with rigor:).

Now there arose up a new king over Egypt, which knew not Joseph the Jew that had led Egypt successfully. And he said unto his people, "behold, the people of the children of Israel are more and mightier than we are". Therefore, they began to deal cruelly with them, lest they multiply, and fight against them, and get them up out of the land. They did set over them taskmasters to afflict them with their burdens. And they built for Pharaoh treasure cities, Pithom and Raamses. But the more they afflicted Israel, the more they multiplied and grew.

Exodus 3v10: (Come now therefore, and I will send thee unto Pharaoh, that thou mayest bring forth my people the children of Israel out of Egypt.)

Moses kept the flock of Jethro his father in law, the priest of Midian: and he led the flock to the backside of the desert, and came to the mountain of Horeb. And the angel of the LORD appeared to him in a flame of fire out of the midst of a bush: and he looked, and, behold, the bush burned with fire, and the bush was not consumed. And Moses turned aside, to see this great sight, why the bush was not burnt. And when the LORD saw that he turned aside to see, God called unto him. And instructed him to go and lead the children of Israel out of slavery. In slavery the Israelites were forced to toil and were treated as products and commodities. The Israelites were enslaved for about 400 years and this brought untold and negative complexes in them.

Exodus 16v3: (And the children of Israel said unto them, Would to God we had died by the hand of the LORD in the land of Egypt, when we sat by the flesh pots, and when we did eat bread to the full; for ye have brought us forth into this wilderness, to kill this whole assembly with hunger.)

God brought Israel out with a mighty hand through the Red sea but a few days after, they began to complain and murmur. A damaged mind doesn't appreciate nor is it grateful. Also, it is quickly given to ideas on death. They said, "that we would have died in the wilderness". It is not progressive but retrogressive. Exodus means departure, Israel departed from Egypt but Egypt didn't depart from them. Departure from slavery alone isn't enough. Egypt haunted their minds for the rest of their lives. God gave Israel manna, an edible substance, in the wilderness. Raw manna tasted like wafers that had been made with honey. They also received water from a rock. God fought for them against their enemies. They received commandments from Him. Quails were provided to them. All these and more wonderful deeds didn't change their minds at all. Israel came out of Egypt with treasure and miracles but their mind was still the same. A slave in the mind is a slave elsewhere. They acquired and obtained abused and warped minds. They had a proclivity to stay in one place-and that is Egypt.

1 Chronicles 4v10: (And Jabez called on the God of Israel, saying, Oh that thou wouldest bless me indeed, and enlarge my coast, and that thine hand might be with me, and that thou wouldest keep me from evil, that it may not grieve me! And God granted him that which he requested.)

Jabez was more honorable than his brethren. His mother called his name Jabez, because he was born with sorrow. His mom allowed the sorrow to name her future. She was ready to memorialize her pain. She was attached to the negative occurrences. Jabez knew that his name would limit his coasts, restrict his blessings and keep him away from God's hand. Therefore, he prayed against the circumstances surrounding his birth. He didn't want to embrace the past into his present and stain his future. Whatever happened to you. Get over it. Envelope yourself in God's love. Don't waste all your life blaming on the way you were raised or born. Major on the major issues than petty ones.

Genesis 35v18: (And it came to pass, as her soul was in departing, (for she died) that she called his name Benoni: but his father called him Benjamin.)

And it came to pass, when Rachel travailed and was in hard labor, that the midwife encouraged her not to fear because she was about to have a son. As she was dying, she called her son Benoni, but his father called him Benjamin. Don't define your blessing by your sorrow. Enjoy your blessing. Don't mix sorrow with the blessing. The negative and temporary situation should not overrule the permanent. Benoni simply means son of my sorrow. But Benjamin means son of my right hand. Right hand represents favor. Favor overcomes sorrow. Let this mind be in you, that of favor. Don't define the rest of your life by a temporary event. There is more to life than that single evil occurrence. Connect yourself to something bigger than your fears.

Genesis 37v10: (And he told it to his father, and to his brethren: and his father rebuked him, and said unto him, What is this dream that thou hast dreamed? Shall I and thy mother and thy brethren indeed come to bow down ourselves to thee to the earth?)

When the brothers learned of the dreams of Joseph they decided to go against him-they had a negative mind. There are people that may act as an obstruction or barrier to your God-given dream. In the case of Job it was the wife, for Jesus it was Judas, for Caleb it was the ten spies, for Nehemiah it was Sanballat, for James it was Herod and for Abel it was Cain as seen in Genesis 4:9. For David it was Absalom and Saul. Your reason for living can be hindered. There is enough reason to win and galvanize your spouse, children, church, organization and any group towards a certain vision. As the adage goes, 'charity begins at home'; we are to win our home before we can win the community. The principle has it that we must win the closest in order to find momentum for the remotest; (Acts 1:8). Start in Jerusalem. Think globally, act locally.

Ephesians 6v12: (For we wrestle not against flesh and blood, but against principalities, against powers, against the rulers of the darkness of this world, against spiritual wickedness in high places.)

Fellow men can be used of the devil to fight against you but we do not fight against flesh nor blood but against principalities. The fact that the brothers are used as agents does not make them targets because they would have subjected themselves to the one that we must fight who is the devil. The anger within you is strategic and should be unleashed towards the devil and if it is wrongly released towards the brothers it does untold harm. The anger is also a sign and indication of your passion, inductively and deductively sense its path and purpose. Without any shadow of doubt, hatred will come along your way to destroy but evade and remain pure from the venom of bitterness. Don't burn your mental energy on anger and negative thoughts. God saw that the wickedness of man was great in the earth, and that every imagination of the thoughts of his heart was only evil continually. Therefore, a flood was brought upon the earth.

Your life's narrative is like a permanent recording playing in your head. Change the negative recording. The negative story of your life is not your future. It is just your story. Therefore, have a life. Snap out of negativity. Most people in prison come from fatherless homes, or a home where a father was emotionally or physically absent. Also, most of them are from homes where abuse was prevalent. The abuse presides as a recording over these minds. The wicked recordings in the mind will ruin your life if permitted to. Put a stop to that rut.

Isaiah 55:7; (Let the wicked forsake his way, and the unrighteous man his thoughts: and let him return unto the Lord, and he will have mercy upon him; and to our God, for he will abundantly pardon.)

Thoughts of man are vanity. History has it and confirms that man's thoughts are evil. Man is troubled by bad thoughts. Some thoughts can lead to Post traumatic conditions. They can lead to a different life all together. A computer virus is a computer program that can replicate itself and spread from one computer to another and may harm a computer system's data or performance. Viruses can enter into our minds and distort our thinking. We need an anti-virus-the word of God. A mind is a garden, it has weeds, snakes and good plants. Cultivate it and till it. Get rid of the weeds. We need a transformative effect from the word. You need to replay in your mind, the events and personal interactions that are important to you and in league with the word. Choose wisely. These recordings will determine your path.

A negative mind has the propensity to blame its excesses, obsessions, rages, tantrums, complexes and behaviors on past experiences but become more than what happened to you. The biggest obstacle to your progress is you. You have to deal with all the forces that pull you down. Forgive yourself of past mistakes, faults and sins-move on. Other people's bad words about you if permitted will mold your life negatively. You have the power to believe or repudiate those words. Forgive those who have hurt you. Strong pictures of the negative past can hinder the prosperous present and future. Your thinking is an appointment or disappointment for your destiny. Thoughts of jealousy, lying, gossip and resentment damage our glands and nerves. They bring physical and mental diseases.

You are not better than your belief system. The evidence that there is prohibited basis information in your mind is reflected by your words and actions. The cancellation of bad thoughts that you have built over a generation cannot be replaced in one day. Rome wasn't built in a day as they say. Work on renewing your mind daily. To the pure all things are pure. Purity gives you another perception that you can't get from impurity. A judgmental mind cannot mix with a peaceful mind, just like oil and water, one has to give-in. You can do a lot more with a mind that is not full of all the negativity, guilt and shame. Take responsibility, all of us are from dysfunctional families. Don't disempower yourself. Don't be self-sabotaging.

Matthew 6:25-27: (*25. Therefore I tell you, do not worry about your life, what you will eat or drink; or about your body, what you will wear. Is not life more important than food and the body more important than clothes? 26. Look at the birds of the air; they do not sow or reap or store away in barns, and yet your heavenly Father feeds them. Are you not much more valuable than they? 27. Who of you by worrying can add a single hour to his life?*)

We spend so much time on worry. We worry about other people, children, parents, school, friends, work, business, the future, money, the unknown and so much more. We are stressed, distressed, troubled and worried. Stress is the number one killer in the world. A study was done on stressed people and the following were the results:

a) They seem to be busy but are not effective.
b) They are angry.
c) They have poor judgement.
d) They have nervous habits.
e) They are impatient.
f) They find it hard to forgive.
g) They don't sleep well.
h) They are very moody.
i) They are quickly irritable.
j) They are mostly rude.

k) They laugh less.
l) They are quickly agitated.
m) They are unfriendly.
n) They feel lonely.
o) They only see the negative.
p) They are quick-tempered.
q) They have memory problems.
r) They have aches and pains.
s) They procrastinate.
t) They are constantly worried.
u) They have racing thoughts.

Adrenalin is given to us for fight and flight, so it's useful for emergencies. But when the adrenalin lingers then it becomes an agent for stress. Our bodies are kept on a treadmill. Some cancers are linked to stress. Stressed people cut the length of their lifespan.

Isaiah 53v2: "For he shall grow up before him as a tender plant, and as a root out of a dry ground: he hath no form nor comeliness; and when we shall see him, there is no beauty that we should desire him."

Unforgiveness keeps us stressed. We need to forgive, it's good for us. Forgiveness is the oil of relationship. He who is devoid of forgiveness is devoid of love. Some of us are still holding and unforgiving of people who died a long time ago. There will always be someone who turns against you, like Judas did to Jesus but we are commanded to forgive them. As Isaiah prophesied that Jesus would grow up as a tender plant and as root out of a dry ground. The dry ground represents negative and difficult circumstances. Sometimes people will contribute to those circumstances but we need to forgive them. Follow peace with all men, think well of them. God has great thoughts about us. Out of the Decalogue or the Ten commandments, four of them deal with our relationship with God. The other six deal with our relationship with people.

The song "it is well with my soul", was written by a Christian lawyer. He had two girls and a wife and the family planned a summer trip to go overseas. Since he had a lot of work to do, he sent his family and decided to follow them latter. He heard the news while on the following ship that another ship had capsized and he knew that his family was there since they mentioned the name of the ship. On his return home, his law firm was burned down and the insurance company refused to pay, they said "it's an act of God". He had no money to pay for his house and no work, he also lost his house. Then while sitting and thinking as to what was happening to him, being a spiritual person, he wrote a song-whatever my Lord, you have taught me to say-it is well, it is well with my soul.

When peace, like a river, attendeth my way,
When sorrows like sea billows roll;
Whatever my lot, thou hast taught me to say,
It is well, it is well with my soul.

It is well with my soul,
It is well, it is well with my soul.

Though Satan should buffet, though trials should come,
Let this blest assurance control,
That Christ has regarded my helpless estate,
And hath shed his own blood for my soul.

My sin, oh, the bliss of this glorious thought!
My sin, not in part but the whole,
Is nailed to the cross, and I bear it no more,
Praise the Lord, praise the Lord, O my soul!

And, Lord, haste the day when my faith shall be sight,
The clouds be rolled back as a scroll;

The trump shall resound, and the Lord shall descend,
Even so, it is well with my soul.

We need to face the negatives in this world with the positives. We overcome evil with good. We are bombarded by negative messages, some driven to us through the medium of technology. The average adult is awake for 16 hours every day and 45 % of that time is spent using a proliferation of technology. 60% of American adults sleep with their cell phones on or right next to their beds. This study shows that 90% reached for their smart phone as the very first thing in the morning. The average teenager sends more than 3,000 texts per month. 42% of Americans say they simply can't live without their cell phones.

Lucille Ball was told that she was not an actor at all. Sir Churchill Winston failed sixth grade and was told that he was not smart. Walt Disney was told by his teacher that he was not creative. Walter Elias "Walt" Disney (December 5, 1901 – December 15, 1966) became an American business magnate, animator, film producer, director, screenwriter, and actor. A major figure within the American animation sector and throughout the world, he is regarded as an international icon, and philanthropist, well known for his influence and contributions. As a Hollywood business mogul, he along with his brother Roy O. Disney, co-founded the Walt Disney Productions, which later became one of the best-known motion picture producers in the world. The corporation had an annual revenue of approximately US$36 billion in the 2010 financial year. He did not hold on to a negative opinion and notion. He was not contained by someone's ideas.

The average person wakes up in the morning with a bad attitude. Statistics show that many people die of heart attacks on a Monday morning between 7 am and 9 am. People don't like what they are doing. They are negative about the world around them. Kids laugh about 50 times a day but adults just laugh about 3 times a day.

Disability inside can cause disability in other areas of life. You can choose to live or leave your past hurts. Shape your life around hope and not hurts. When there is no enemy inside, the enemy outside can't hurt you. Judas and Peter rejected Christ but Peter came back. You are not what you did or what happened to you. The mind of man is the battleground on which every moral and spiritual battle is fought. Losing the battle of the mind leads to missing the mark or sin. Sin alienates us from God, from others and from us. We need God to be whole. We need to be at one with self, others and God. Don't create a foundation and a building of your life based on what naysayers think about you, this will tear you apart and break your focus.

Intoxicated thinking doesn't line up with God's ways. We must be sure to evict this type of thinking and embrace the mind of Christ. Sin destroys our minds and it distorts our perception. Legion was in his right mind after Jesus had cast out the devils. Don't be entangled in a web of negativity. No matter how sharp the hurt, it should not barricade you from your destiny. Your body was not designed to handle negative emotions, like anger, suspicion, jealousy, mistrust and bitterness. Bitterness destroys optimism and faith. So, the body pushes those reactions to a leeway, for example the stomach. People begin to have ulcers due to these emotions. If you don't want to live a trash life, don't pile trash in your mind. Your impact is limited by you. Fight against negative stereotypes. There is no time to be sorry for yourself. Forgiveness isn't a suggestion but a requirement.

If you are going through hell, you should not sink. Simply put one foot in front of the other and continue to move. Don't focus on the problem but on the way forward. You are a fruitful bough planted by the well and your branches go over the wall like Joseph who endured all the negativity on his way to premiership. The devil wanted to have the Apostle Peter to sift him as wheat but Jesus prayed for him that his faith would not fail. Don't entertain a negative mind because you are going through. Our minds are our servants. We can use them for good or evil.

It's unhealthy and sickly to tolerate drama in your life. Arguments, altercations and contentions create dis-ease and abnormal conditions. Remove yourself away from negative, selfish, energy-draining relationships that do not honor you. Those that abuse and take advantage of your kindness. Don't buy into their negativity or guilt trips. Guilt trips are so expensive. A negative state of mind will produce negative conditions which are not conducive for production and creativity. Make a solid resolution to live in peace. Don't try to change others. There is enough work to do on yourself. You are a work in progress. Develop relationships where all parties can grow and create an atmosphere of mutual respect, love, and appreciation. Free yourself from inner chaos by meditation, relaxation and stillness. What you create inside of yourself will manifest outside ultimately. Create a sanctuary where you can live in peace, relax your mind, revive your spirit and renew your purpose. Your happiness is your responsibility. Enjoy your life. You are created for a higher purpose and calling.

When you are traumatized by a certain situation, you can be frozen in that state of mind and it may affect the way you perceive things for a lifetime, if you allow it. A person going through divorce for example can be so traumatized by it that they go into their next marriage with a defensive mentality of not wanting to be hurt again. Their state of mind is not balanced at all. They judge the present by the negative past to their detriment. Life approached with a timid mind that is afraid of being hurt again will not have impact and energy. The internal strength is reduced. Don't normalize your trauma. Approach each day with freshness. God's mercies are new every morning. There is new manna for today. Don't be afraid of pain. No pain, no gain. Be ready to confront the day with a new perspective. Don't fear your fears. Overcome your tragedies. Get the closure you need. Don't nurse a wound for decades. Marriage involves the social, physical, intellectual, spiritual and financial parts of us. So, when you divorce, a lot of energy is lost into it and that can be devastating. It will cost you so much to go through the situation. But recover from your emotional tiredness. Don't mistreat people based on your past injuries. Don't fight against yourself. A judgmental thought process closes doors for us. It makes us to see people in a wrong way. Our perception is warped, eccentric and kinked. Judgmental people don't succeed easily because they cannot even learn from anyone. You can't celebrate what you criticize.

Injecting trash into your mind is like putting junk food into your body. Junk food does not strengthen the physical body, rather it makes its immunity weak against diseases. The same goes for the mind. Don't produce a weak mind by what you feed it. You take your car for an oil change periodically because you want to prevent seizure, knock, damage and dysfunction to your motor. The same goes for your mind. It needs constant maintenance. As long as we continue to think in terms of average camps, with reasoning tainted by the cult of blame, we will do very little to address the monumental challenges facing our lives. We cannot continue to blame as if this will bring a solution to the crisis in our backyards. No more stereotypes in your life. Break the labels, no more chip on your shoulder. No contamination from your past will derail God's purpose.

People who overcame negativity.

Colonel Sanders : *The founder of KFC. He started his dream and vision at 66 years old! He got a social security check for only $105 and was angry. Instead of complaining he was proactive. KFC had sales of $23 billion in 2013.*

Tyler Perry: *In 1998, he channeled all his savings into the making of a play. It was a failure and Perry ended up with nothing and living on the street. He kept showing the play in churches and working jobs* until he got his breakthrough. Forbes listed him as the highest paid man in entertainment in 2011, making $130 million that year alone.

Walt Disney: His first company went bankrupt. He was fired for lack of imagination.

Oprah Winfrey: She was fired from her position at a local news station. Today, she is one of the richest women in the world.

Albert Eistein: He didn't speak till he was four and didn't read till seven. His parents and teachers thought he was mentally handicapped.

Mark Cuban: He was terrible at his early jobs. He tried carpentry but hated it. He waited tables but couldn't open a bottle of wine.

John Grisham: The American author. His first book A Time to Kill took 3 years to write. The book was rejected 28 times until he got one yes. He's sold over 250 million copies of his books.

Vincent Van Gogh: He only sold one painting in his lifetime! Despite that he kept painting and finished over 800 pieces. Now everyone wants to buy them and his most expensive painting is valued at $142.7 million.

Steven Spielberg: He applied and was denied two times to the University of Southern California film school. Instead he went to Cal State University in Long Beach. He went on to direct some of the biggest movie blockbusters in history. Now he's worth $2.7 billion and in 1994 got an honorary degree from the film school that rejected him twice.

Bishop TD Jakes: When he was young, he was told that he could not be a preacher because he had a lisp or a speech impediment. But he is now a founder and preacher of a 30,000 member church and of the Mega Fest conference that draws about 100,000 people. Do not believe a lie. God can use you despite that challenge.

CHAPTER TEN

THE MINDSET

'Never give in' was my mindset'. Unknown

Isaiah 26:3: (Thou wilt keep him in perfect peace, whose mind is stayed on thee: because he trusteth in thee.)

The mind can be set hence the word "mindset". When a brick is set in cement, it becomes almost impossible to pull them apart. The same goes for thoughts that are set in the soils of our minds. The good news is that you have the ability to set the tone of your mind. You can change your life by altering your mind. People work less at their workplaces on weekends because they set their minds on a go-slow mode. Tune your mind by letting go of yesterday's negative thoughts. Don't create your future based on your toxic thoughts. Shifting is hard for people because of preconceptions. Knowledge can change the mindset. Your mind is a magnet-so set it right so that it can attract the right things. Garbage-in, garbage-out is a known phrase that represents the fact that what we take in is what we produce, but also the remnants of that garbage stays in our mind. A mind set on garbage will produce garbage at all cost. Refuse to admit information that stains your mind in a bad way. The garbage in the recesses of the mind will affect the setting of the mind. We cannot choose our birthday or our death-day, but we can choose in our mind how we live in between the two. We can choose what we allow on the voice mail of our thoughts. Don't play old, negative, toxic thoughts in your mind. We cannot always control situations but we can always control our thoughts. Choose healthy and not toxic thoughts.

Psalm 119v11:(I have hidden your word in my heart, that I might not sin against you).

We all need to vacuum our minds daily with the word of God. Get rid of the proverbial rust of the mind. David made God's word to sit and settle in his heart. A settled word in the heart creates a settled mind. Develop a way of thinking in league with God. Positive thoughts bring progress and not retrogression. Align your thinking and your lifestyle will fall in place with God's plan. Your mindset can pull you back into Egypt or forward into Canaan. Oppression removed the ability from Israel to control their own future. The repetition of the word of God brings a paradigm shift or a radical change in underlying beliefs. There are basic, fundamental, lying under or beneath beliefs that make or break us. It is not easy to change beliefs in our minds. It requires strong conviction in God's word. The word hid in our hearts will deal with the corruption. Let the word deal with your sub-conscious mind.

Being victorious or not is a mindset. A mind poised on excellence is a powerful asset. Mindsets can send messages for us to perceive things differently according to our training and conditioning. It's not an easy task to change your mindset-but it's beneficial. Commitment to renew the mindset will pay dividends. Businesses, Universities, athletes, coaches, Navy Seals-all these operate and function at the rate, speed and level of their mindsets. About 25% of those who go through the Navy Seal training make it per year. The training is arduous both physically and mentally. They are trained to endure harsh times. The mind should be trained not to have a propensity and inclination to failure but success. Being stuck in an old mindset can retard forward movement. Reset your mindset. You can't change your state of mind in one day. It is a protracted process.

The change of a mindset is the change of your world. It takes a different mindset to be successful-that is why in many cases all over the world only a minority control the majority of the wealth and resources. The minority would have taken time to set their minds so as to speak, and they prosper. Companies like Yahoo, Google, Microsoft and others have environments that urge creative thinking that brings invention and innovation. Self-doubt is a sign of an untrained mindset. It's not just about the opportunity but the mindset. Make the best out of every moment. Live life to the full.

Deception is a trick, fraud, falseness, concealment or distortion of the truth for the purpose of misleading. Many of us have believed a lie and we are being misled. Deception will lead and guide us wrongly. What type of lie is leading you into error of conduct, thought and judgement? If a majority believes a lie that doesn't make it truth. Believing a lie for a long time doesn't make it the truth either. No matter how much energy you spend on believing a lie, that will not set you free. The devil twists the truth out of shape, makes it crooked and perverted. God has an original intended purpose for your life but it has been misshaped, misrepresented and altered out of shape. The devil doesn't only lie but is the progenitor of all lies. He originates and directs all lies. He can make a lie become a reality. The devil makes false statements with deliberate intent to deceive you out of your blessing. You are not a mistake. You are not a failure. You are not a loser. You are not weak. You are not sick. You are not suicidal. You are not about to die. You are not confused. Know the truth and it will set you free. You are free!!!!!!. Out of 7.1 billion people in the whole world, God chose you. You are unique.

Business cannot thrive under a mindset full of failure. Strive to thrive by changing it. A mindset submerged in suspicion will extend it's tentacles and become suspicious even of success. A negative mindset hinders creativity because the source of all creativity and creation is God and God is pure. Lock the door to negative influence of the past. Make it a point to mediate not only on the fact that God is with you but that he is for you. Remember that God uses heat, pressure and time to create diamonds, in both humans and rocks. Nothing changes in our lives until our minds change. When you go through the heat that should not make you bitter but better. Have a mindset with a mission. Keep a focused perspective as you go through life.

Your disposition determines your position. Your attitude determines your altitude. Your inclination determines your increase. Your propensity determines your possession. Change the negative predominant and prevailing tendencies in your mind. We all have a tendency to act in a certain way. The intense and natural inclinations or preferences should align with the word of God. What kind of thoughts are you prone to?. The answer to that question depicts your mindset. The habitual attraction, affinity and aptitude control the path of your life. Be bent towards the noble. Have a proclivity for worthy thoughts. The likelihood for your thoughts to become future actions is very high unless an interception occurs. The mental house should be occupied by excellent thoughts. Meditation on God's word evicts the devilish thoughts from your mind. Employ your mind to some good use. After the fall of man, the human mind became self-destroying and self-sabotaging. We need salvation to solve that problem of depravity.

Outside conditions cannot influence your life without your consent. You have the power to influence your life through your mindset. You will reach the altitude of your strongest desires. You attract what is deeply embedded and ingrained in you. Meditation and cogitation build thoughts to their highest level of maturity and they break forth into manifestation. Setting your mind to a certain level creates the particular and equivalent inclination. Good thoughts are the means to a good end. Having evil thoughts and expecting a good end is deception and it's against the law of thought. The solution to an enslaved mentality is the hearkening to God's word. Meditation on God's word removes the tattoos of failure from our minds. The word sets us free. Create a habit of meditating on the word. The 613 commandments of God in the Torah created habits for the children of Israel. What we do daily will affect our destiny. A wrong opinion about God will hurt you. God is not out to get you but to bless you. Change your thinking about God. Do the following in order to renew your mind:

a) Confess the word of God on a daily basis.
b) Think noble thoughts on purpose and intentionally.
c) Believe the word of God.
d) Study the word of God.
e) Meditate on the word of God.
f) Pray scripturally.
g) Do the word of God.
h) Control your eye and ear gates.
i) Learn from others who are greater than you.
j) Invest in great books.
k) Attend anointed, inspiring and informative seminars, conferences and meetings.
l) Find every possible way to upgrade yourself in your area of expertise.
m) Have a room with the photographs of your future. Look at them daily.
n) Have think sessions- On a daily basis, make an effort to allocate some time completely for thinking. Start with a few minutes a day, and add them as you see fit and reasonable.

CHAPTER ELEVEN

THINK BIG

The biggest obstacle to wealth is fear. People are afraid to think big, but if you think small, you'll only achieve small things. T. Harv Eker

"Consider this: we could travel off of this planet in any direction at the speed of light, 186,000 miles a second, for billions of years, and never begin to exhaust what we already know to exist. All of that rests in the palm of His hand. And it is this God who wants to fill us with His fullness. That ought to make a difference!" — Bill Johnson

Genesis 15v5: (And he brought him forth abroad, and said, Look now toward heaven, and tell the stars, if thou be able to number them: and he said unto him, So shall thy seed be).

How big is your fight against smallness? Are you average or below standard in terms of the size and magnitude of your dream? Make a stand, dig in and never give up. Don't be afraid of failure, fail forward. Failure is feedback. Try one more time, persistence pays. Success doesn't come by accident-prepare to win. Thinking big pulls you from an underdog status to notoriety. Don't just concentrate on strengthening your strengths but strengthening your weaknesses too towards big thinking and accomplishments. God wanted Abraham to see and conceive the fact that he is a patriarch, a father of multitudes. Abraham was stretched by looking at the trillions of stars. He received the promised child at a 100 years. God asked Abraham to count the stars and he couldn't do it because they were so many. There is so much more in store for you. Too many stars are unfathomable but not impossible oh Abraham. Great and mighty things await you.

1 Corinthians 2v9: (But as it is written, Eye hath not seen, nor ear heard, neither have entered into the heart of man, the things which God hath prepared for them that love him).

God has prepared things that are well above our senses. If you buy a black Mercedes Benz 500 s, you begin to see more of those cars because your awareness would have been opened to that aspect. There is a sleeping awareness that we awaken and evoke as we travel and get exposed. There are many opportunities that are available but hidden till we can see them. Fully occupy the space that God has made available for you. David the shepherd boy had the capacity to be the king of Israel, Moses the murderer had the capacity to be a deliverer, Saul had the capacity to be Apostle Paul who wrote about two thirds of the New testament. Gideon the fearful had the capacity to be a leader and a great fighter. Increase your depth in everything you do. Yesterday's success could hinder you from going up to the next level. New and great thinking produce new possibilities. Fossilized and antiquated minds can make your life outmoded or inflexible with time. Think outside the experiences of your life. Re-orient your mind to accommodate greatness. Alignment and adjustment are essential for upward and onward movement.

Romans 4v19: (And being not weak in faith, he considered not his own body now dead, when he was about an hundred years old, neither yet the deadness of Sarah's womb):

Abraham did not consider, contemplate or think of the deadness of Sarah's womb. Don't consider your situation but consider Jesus the author and finisher of your faith. If you consider your current situation, you abort your miracle. Considering your situation blocks your destiny. It is a fact that Sarah's womb was as good as dead but Abraham saw beyond that and he got great results. Abraham thought carefully, deliberated and pondered on the promises. What are you taking into account on your situation? Thoughts would come to Abraham about Sarah's womb but he did not cogitate on them. If you reflect on the deadness, you get nothing out of it. Sarah had a dead womb and Abraham was old, a complicated situation and equation but God solved it. Considering the dead womb will not change its state. But considering God will resurrect the dead womb. Considering God changes our vantage point. It might be a hard situation but possible all the same.

Set your sight up. Aim high. Don't aim too low and hit. Aim at the stars so that if you miss you can land somewhere high in the sky. If you don't think anything big, small achievements will satisfy you. Thinking is hard work. Steve Jobs was fired at Apple. He came back to Apple and changed the world because he was a big and generational thinker. Generational thinkers are not mediocre in their planning. They have a cause and a reason that direct their paths. They are miles away from the enslavement caused by the opinions of the naysayers. Ideas are what they feed on. They capitalize even on ordinary talents and bring gold out of it. They are ordinary people who put an extraordinary effort to produce extraordinary results. They go through remarkable pressure but are not bitter, instead they are better. They don't retain offenses. Offenses harbored can contaminate your thinking.

The prodigal son was reckless and myopic. He did not think big, he didn't have the big picture. He could not envision his bliss at his dad's house. His thoughts led him to a foolish decision and request. The very same thoughts projected into wild living could have been converted and aimed towards successful living. He spent all and was left with nothing-his mind was not trained for increase. He starved to death. He was glad to eat with the pigs. A Jewish man would have felt terribly insulted if he had to feed pigs, much less eat with them. He was so low to the point of losing his self-esteem. After a while he came back to his senses. He declared that he had sinned against his father and God. When he returned to his father, he received new clothes, shoes, a ring and the best calf was prepared. His return led to celebration and feasting.

Scarcity is the fundamental and basic problem of having seemingly unlimited human wants and needs in a world of limited resources. Scarcity mentality makes people think or see little in life. Fight your way away from the comfort zone of smallness and begin to reign supreme in large thinking. Discard low thinking. Resist to be an average thinker and pull yourself up from the unworthy surroundings. Think big and grow big. Be a skilled thinker who sees what others don't see. Through the ideas of big thinkers in the health sector, in one century, 28 years have been added to the average life span in the USA. In a world of dire straits, thinkers breakthrough the barriers and do the impossible. Don't live in the status quo. Redeem yourself from the stereotypes, there is more. A stereotype is a thought that may be adopted about specific types of individuals or certain ways of doing things, but that belief may or may not accurately reflect reality. Change the evil record that is playing in your mind because it will affect your life for the worst. Make no acknowledgement of regret for the pursuit of your greatest life. A life larger than you.

1 Chronicles 4:10: (And Jabez called on the God of Israel, saying, Oh that thou wouldest bless me indeed, and enlarge my coast, and that thine hand might be with me, and that thou wouldest keep me from evil, that it may not grieve me! And God granted him that which he requested.)

"Enlarge my territory". God is increasing your territory. Be allergic to smallness. Your dream is greater than just average. Stretch yourself beyond mediocrity. You cannot have large territories by making simple decisions only, dare to make complex decisions. You are transitioning from poverty to plenty." Lord that you would bless me indeed". The word "bless" means to boost. God is boosting, refueling, recharging and reloading your life, business, marriage, ministry, gifts, family and church. The boost is resurrecting that dead situation and removing the curse and pain from your name, oh Jabez.

This is a list of the different types of people. I would rather be a thinker who leaves an indelible mark on the earth.
a) Drinkers-earn a lot of knowledge but don't turn it into wisdom.
b) Believers-they only believe but have no accompanying works. Even devils believe.
c) Watchers-they don't want to participate, they just watch.
d) Wishers-they die wishing. If wishes were horses, beggars would ride.
e) Hangers-they hang their ideas. The idea isn't good until it's used.
f) Philosophers-they only interpret the world but don't change it.
g) Talkers-they just talk it and never walk it.
h) Pokers-they are always instigating trouble.
i) Magicians-they believe that everything is self-driven-automated.
j) Gossipers-they are small minds that always discuss people.
k) Procrastinators-they do things tomorrow that should be done today.
l) Admirers-they just admire others.
m) Cankers-these cause damage to the team.
n) Abandoners-they tolerate rather than celebrate your dream.

o) Abasers-they reduce you to a lower point.
p) Abuser-they use and mistreat you.
q) Accuser-they charge you with a wrongdoing.
r) Blubbers-they always sob noisily but never change.
s) Misers-they don't contribute to your dream.
t) Killers-they destroy your dream.
u) Thinkers-they leave a ding on the world.

Life is calling you up higher. Continue to make extra strides and rise to the occasion. Before you die, live.

CHAPTER TWELVE

A FOCUSED MIND

Thinking is the hardest work there is, which is probably the reason why so few engage in it. Henry Ford

2 Peter 1v19: (We have also a more sure word of prophecy; whereunto ye do well that ye take heed, as unto a light that shineth in a dark place, until the day dawn, and the day star arise in your hearts:)

Don't let your thoughts wander aimlessly. Converge all your thoughts upon the targeted work at hand. The sun's rays do not burn until they are drawn to a focus. Focus like a laser beam until you get what you want. You should be able to write your mission statement at the back of a business card. It should be brief and precise. Clarity of mission eradicates confusion. If you think of Tiger Woods, immediately golf comes in mind. If you think of Steve Jobs, Apple Inc comes in mind. If we reflect on Oral Roberts, teaching on seed-time harvest comes to mind. If we think of Myles Munroe, we can't just afford not to think of the teaching on purpose. Mike Murdock's name is linked to wisdom. Benny Hinn's name is connected to the healing ministry. Pat Robertson name is synonymous with CBN. Joel Osteen's name is connected to uplifting and motivational messages. TD Jakes's name is connected to Mega Fest. Paul Crouch's name is married to TBN. Marcus Lamb's name is one with Daystar. Kenneth Copeland, Jerry Savelle, Creflo Dollar and Jesse Duplantis are known for faith and abundance teachings. Nelson Mandela, the anti-apartheid hero, admired across the world. He is synonymous of a symbol of resistance against injustice and oppression and then of racial reconciliation. Every successful person is linked to one thing that they can do so well a cut above the average. Be a master in one area. If we learn from these mentors we would have given ourselves the greatest of education. Give yourself wholly to your purpose. If you intentionally make focus a habit it will become second nature to you. Success in its highest and noblest form demands the use of focus. Don't spread your energy over many things lest all be watered down. When we focus we do the ordinary extraordinarily well. Power lies in consistent focus. Obsession precedes possession. Don't be more obsessed by obstacles than by opportunities. Success and greatness are expensive. Greatness doesn't go on sale. Don't spread yourself too thin.

Set objectives for yourself. Think about things you have always wanted to achieve, and work industriously towards them. We learn and produce better when we are interested. This will give focus to your creativity. Focus helps you to process your thoughts deeply. Distraction is a hindrance to creative thinking. Live, breathe, talk, dream, focus and zero in on the success in your selected area. Every great achievement and work has been done by focused minds. And we have the firm prophetic word of God still. You will do well to focus on it as to a lamp shining in a dismal, squalid and dark place, until the day breaks through the gloom in your hearts.

John9v25: (He answered and said, Whether he be a sinner or no, I know not: one thing I know, that, whereas I was blind, now I see.)

Focus is when all lines seem to be centered on one point and so as to form a high concentration. The headlights of an automobile are focused to ensure safety especially during rainy and dark times. If the headlights are not focused they are weak, diluted and just spread all over the place. Focus increases the intensity and strength. Focus brings stability and one does not waver. Focus creates a willingness to see the end. Hope and joy is a result of focus. The focused people will always finish the race and not just necessarily run. Many medical researchers focus on studying and finding a cure for a single and particular disease for so many years. In John 9, the person who was given sight by Jesus was interrogated by the Sanhedrin which was a council that was against Jesus. This council was amazed at the response of the man because he said 'All I know is that I was blind but now I see', this is focus. He didn't allow the naysayers to dissuade him out of his blessing. He kept his particular course of action without being affected by the critics or by those who expressed unfavorable opinions.

We are overcome by temptation due to lack of focus and the devil capitalizes on this. This man did not get out from the parameters of his knowledge of what had happened to him at the mercy of the evil council. Stick to the knowledge and preeminence of Christ and the enemy will falter. In Acts 20v24, Paul was told by a genuine prophet, Agabus, that he was going to be imprisoned in Jerusalem. This prophetic utterance was enacted by the prophet but did not stop Paul from going to Jerusalem. Paul was not only willing to be imprisoned but to die. Paul wanted to finish his race well and to keep the faith. Paul had a deep conviction and this is why he was not moved by the circumstances. Mathew 13:45, teaches us that a Merchant sold all he had in order to buy one pearl of great value. Sell all in order to buy one and focus on that. Don't be a jack of all trades because it pays more to specialize. Thomas Edison said "I'm not smarter but I think of one thing all day".

Mathew 14v28: (And Peter answered him and said, Lord, if it be thou, bid me come unto thee on the water).

The ship was now in the middle of the sea, tossed with waves: for the wind was contrary. And in the fourth watch of the night Jesus went unto them, walking on the sea. And when the disciples saw him walking on the sea, they were troubled, saying, It is a spirit; and they cried of fear. But Jesus spoke unto them to be not afraid. Peter asked the lord to bid him to come on water if it was truly him. Jesus answered him and said, come. Peter came down out of the ship, and walked on the water, to go to Jesus. But when he saw the wind boisterous, he was afraid; and began to sink, he cried, for the Lord to save him. Immediately Jesus stretched his hand, and caught him. When Peter focused on Christ and not the water, he walked on it. The water was boisterous and the wind was blowing but that was not his focus. Focus keeps you walking. It makes you see and experience miracles. The seas can't drown a focused Peter. Allowing the outside noise into you, triggers the sinking to begin. You are propelled by what you see. What you see drowns or sustains you. What you see produces your miracle or your mishap. Peter paid attention to the circumstance and he went under it. Focus and measure your progress regularly. You live at the level of the knowledge you focus on. Singleness of purpose is a prerequisite for our prosperity in all of life's areas. A research concluded that reading 60 applicable books in a specific area will make you an expert. This would require for you to read one book per month for 5 years. Focus till you become an expert in a certain area. Specialists in particular areas earn more than those who just generalize. Thomas A. Edison said, "I have not failed. I've just found 10,000 ways that won't work". Edison was after one thing, the bulb. Focus on what you want to know a lot about. Consciously focus on things you desire not fear. Einstein famously said "it's not that I'm smart, it's just that I stay with the problems longer".

Luke 9v62: (And Jesus said unto him, No man, having put his hand to the plough, and looking back, is fit for the kingdom of God.)

Focused people look forward and not backwards. Having your hand on the plough and looking back is unfit for God's kingdom. Looking back cuts into your production to reduce it. There is a coordination between your work, focus and profitability. They that focus are suitable and will produce. The land has stones, weeds, stumps of old tree roots, hard places but the farmer should focus and push through with his plough in such places. Looking back with your hand on the plough causes imbalance. There are some places that require more strength on your part than others and if you look back then disaster is inevitable.

Genesis 19v26: (But his wife looked back from behind him, and she became a pillar of salt.)

Lot and his family were commanded not to look back. But Lot's wife looked back and she became a pillar of salt. Looking back turned her into nothing useful. The rest of the family focused and won against destruction and consumption. God was raining brimstone and fire upon Sodom and Gomorrah out of heaven; And was overthrowing the cities, and all the plain, and all the inhabitants of the cities, and that which grew upon the ground. And Lot's wife had no business in looking back. Distraction stopped and destroyed her right in her tracks. The children became motherless because of her decision to backslide. Our decisions to go back affect our families, communities, churches, companies, organizations and countries at large. Lets set our minds on going forward.

Phillipians 3v13: (Brethren, I count not myself to have apprehended: but this one thing I do, forgetting those things which are behind, and reaching forth unto those things which are before,)

Psalm 27:4 (One thing have I desired of the Lord, that will I seek after; that I may dwell in the house of the Lord all the days of my life, to behold the beauty of the Lord, and to enquire in his temple.)

Apostle Paul and David proclaimed "this one thing". Concentrate on the one thing and you will realize the success that comes out of it. Focus will make you to drive even better results. The fewer the words of the vision, the better. Focus on a vision and success will rush to fill the proverbial vacuum as it were. Focus gives us the competitive advantage. Be fully persuaded of one thing till it comes to pass. The average attention span for a man is twenty five minutes but habitual focus can improve it. Concentrate your power and energy. Master one thing. Make an emphasis on one area. The secret to success is taking and gathering all scattered pieces of energy into one. We need relentless focus. Unlocking the full potential requires focus. Total focus produces total success. Lack of focus births generalizations. Focus births specificity. All energy concentrated on one thing will produce tremendous results. Apostle Paul said that he forgets the past and reaches for things ahead of him. Go past your past.

1 Samuel 17v26: (And David spake to the men that stood by him, saying, What shall be done to the man that killeth this Philistine, and taketh away the reproach from Israel? for who is this uncircumcised Philistine, that he should defy the armies of the living God?

Diverted energy accomplishes little. You cannot focus on your future and your past simultaneously. The principle is that what we focus on intensifies. Specific focus creates spacious faith. David focused on the rewards and he killed Goliath. It's easy to shake off someone's faith in himself but David refused to admit to failure. See what is ahead of you and you will overcome obstacles. David focused on his goals.

Goals are expandable and thereby can expand your territory. Knowing your goal is a great percentage of the work done. Goals have the ability to reprogram the clock of your life. Have goals and plan. Those who fail to plan, plan to fail.

James 1v6-8: (But let him ask in faith, nothing wavering. For he that wavereth is like a wave of the sea driven with the wind and tossed. For let not that man think that he shall receive any thing of the Lord. A double minded man is unstable in all his ways.)

A double-minded or a two-minded person will not succeed in anything. Singularity of mind is key to our success. A double-minded person is also double-tongued. Don't change your confession, stick to it. Your mind should withstand the tempest of the seas. Don't be driven by every wind of doctrine. A double-minded person blocks his miracles because he cannot receive anything from God. Our minds should be sound in a world full of turbulence. Focus is what we need. Distraction is the main cause of failure. Just imagine what you could do with a focused mind. How much would you accomplish if you would strive after one thing. Keep the main thing as the main thing. Don't major on minors. An athlete loses his forward stride by looking back. Don't look back, don't falter. Forward is the theme-towards one thing, mission, vision, objective, goal and dream. Specialization or pursuing a specific line of business is the way to go even in big corporations in the twenty first century. Starbucks has generally become a billion dollar business from selling coffee-their focus is coffee. Everyone has a destiny but it cannot be reached by double-mindedness.

Mathew 6v33: (But seek ye first the kingdom of God, and his righteousness; and all these things shall be added unto you).

Focus on the kingdom of God primarily. The primary will lead to the secondary and not vice-versa. So putting first things first will make us win. Putting the secondary as the first will make us lose the primary which is God's kingdom. Priority is the key to resounding success-doing everything in the order of importance. The primary will sustain the rest. Anything foundational will support the rest of the building. Put God first and He will bring and attract all that you need. If God is put first, he will bring all things you need but if 'all things' are put first then God will not be in it. When you put God first, then you will not chase stuff but attract them.

Recent research shows that multitasking gets less done when applied to practical life. You are wired to deal with one problem at a time. When you give attention to one thing, it is done effectively, efficiently, excellently and exceptionally. Don't allow your life to be full of distractions, chatter and noise. This will sway you from real achievement. The use of Mobile phones while driving is common in nowadays, but widely and strongly considered harmful. Due to the number of accidents that are related to cell phone use while driving, some jurisdictions have made the use of a cell phone while driving illegal. Others have enacted laws to ban handheld mobile phone use, but allow the use of a hands free device. This study shows the power of focus. Our minds wander because of distractions. This is a world full of noise, chatter and clamor. Take responsibility for your habits and focus on what you can do to change them.

Summary points
- Don't let your thoughts wander aimlessly.
- Focus like a laser beam until you get what you want.
- Clarity of mission eradicates confusion.
- Success in its highest and noblest form demands the use of focus.
- Every successful person is linked to one thing that they can do so well.
- When you give attention to one thing, it is done effectively, efficiently, excellently and exceptionally.

CHAPTER THIRTEEN

THE MIND AND SPEAKING

Think twice before you speak, because your words and influence will plant the seed of either success or failure in the mind of another. Napoleon Hill

Revelation 12v11:(And they overcame him by the blood of the Lamb, and by the word of their testimony; and they loved not their lives unto the death.)

Words are a projection and extension of your thoughts. Change the way you speak and think. Believe what you say, and also what God says. You get what you say. Say what God says, do what God does. Words go to the root. They kill or nurture the root. We conquer the devil by means of the blood of the Lamb and by the utterance of our mouths. Right words and thoughts are forceful. Speak right. Negative words will hinder the pictures and the promises of God in your spirit. We overcome by our testimony. Bad words create thought-bombs in our thinking that detonate and destroy our lives.

Mark 11v20: (And in the morning, as they passed by, they saw the fig tree dried up from the roots).

And seeing a fig tree afar off having leaves, Jesus came, if he might find anything on it: and when he came to it, he found nothing but leaves; for the time of figs was not yet. Jesus spoke that no man would eat fruit from it forever. On the next day as they passed, they saw the fig tree dried up from the roots. Jesus's words dried up the roots of the tree. The words sapped the life out of the tree. Words are equated to results, whether positive or negative. Words are active which means they are as powerful as actions.

Proverbs 18v21:(Death and life are in the power of the tongue: and they that love it shall eat the fruit thereof.)

Romans 10vv17:(So then faith cometh by hearing, and hearing by the word of God.)

Life and death is in the power of the tongue. Speak life. Situations may be dead but you can speak life and resurrection to them. The choice is yours. Death cannot withstand the words of faith and life from your mouth. Speak life. There are fruits from the words that we speak. The worlds were created by words from God's mouth. The visible and the invisible were created by words. We can create with our words too. Continue to speak because faith cometh by hearing and hearing and persistent hearing. Hearing the word repeatedly produces active faith. As you speak you also hear yourself.

Psalms 118v17: (I shall not die, but live, and declare the works of the LORD.)

Whatever you speak is reinforced in you. Speaking is likened to a pen. What you speak, you write. God spoke light into being. You are ordained to decree and pronounce as per the desired end. Visionaries speak vision. Psalms 118:17 is a Psalm that was sung by Jesus at the Passover. A little time before his death. He sang that he was not going to die but live and declare God's works. He saw beyond the cross and the many souls to be saved. You inevitably become what you think and what you think is partly contributed by your words. What you think you believe and what you believe you behave. Scientists have discovered that the purest form of DNA is in the mouth and this implicitly means that your words have a bearing on your identity. Your words represent your personality. The purest identity is in your mouth. Never say that it will not work. Never say that you can't do it. Do not bewitch yourself by your words. James shows us that words can be used for cursing and for blessing. Negative words bring stagnation. We shackle ourselves through our words and thoughts-release yourself. It is well.

Deuteronomy 4v30: (When thou art in tribulation, and all these things are come upon thee, even in the latter days, if thou turn to the LORD *thy God, and shalt be obedient unto his voice).*

We are made for conversations. God does a lot of speaking. Jesus was always speaking. God speaks and we do the same to him, we have a dialogue with Him and not a monologue. Conversation is the basis for understanding. Talk to yourself-you are the only one that can really talk to you. You can talk to yourself into misery or out of it. Master self-talk. Your tongue is connected to your emotions. Conversation is a factory for your future. They say every thought you have recurs about 100 times, so displace it by speaking God's word repeatedly. Daily renew your mind by speaking Gods word. Use the law of displacement, get rid of the trash by using his word. What you speak is the seed for the next level. Your future is hidden in moments, change your moments through speaking wisdom. Believe what you say. Lawyers and motivational speakers are paid for speaking. You get what you say. You live what you planted yesterday through your words. What we hear from our speaking is integrated with what we have heard before, therefore forming a cumulative effect. Adam named the animals, name and speak to your environment. David named Goliath as an opportunity. God renamed Golgotha as the landmark of salvation of mankind. Your mind can re-size your opponent as grasshoppers or as giants. Just as some snakes have venom in their mouths, poison from the evil words in your mouth can kill and bewitch you. Speak the word. Speak life. Speak against that disease, death, poverty, anger using God's word in your mouth.

Genesis 2:7: (And the LORD God formed man of the dust of the ground and breathed into his nostrils the breath of life; and man became a living soul.)

The LORD God took a handful of soil and made a man. God breathed life into the man, and the man started breathing or became a living and speaking being. We are speakers. We speak things into being. We are creative through words. We should have alignment between what we think, say and do. You can undo a great prayer by your negative mouth. What you say can and will be used against you. You have the right to choose your words and thoughts. Your words should not be idle, unemployed, un-operational, un-intended, because we will be judged by God for them.

Mark 11v23-24: (For verily I say unto you, That whosoever shall say unto this mountain, Be thou removed, and be thou cast into the sea; and shall not doubt in his heart, but shall believe that those things which he saith shall come to pass; he shall have whatsoever he saith. Therefore I say unto you, What things soever ye desire, when ye pray, believe that ye receive them, and ye shall have them.

What you speak you own, negative or positive. "Whatever you say", appears three times in this portion of scripture. Believe what he says about you even if it's beyond the natural realm and human conception. What you believe empowers you to become. Watch what you say-it will come to pass. Words are creative. We can create the bad or the good. There are words everywhere, from the books, televisions, other people and radios. But we need to choose the best of words. With the same mouth we bless God but we also have the temptation to curse with the same mouth. Fresh and brackish or briny water can come from the same mouth. The spirit of faith is a speaking spirit. The more you talk about your negative situations, the more that situation increases. Your words are sculpturing your world. Get your words going in the right direction and your life will follow. Your words betray and portray the true picture of your mind. One's character can be studied by the vocabulary he constantly uses.

Defend your mind by confessing God's word in the morning, afternoon and evening. Elisha the protégé of Elijah asked for a double portion of the anointing and he received it. He received in accordance to his plea and words. He did exactly double the miracles of Elijah. Elisha's last miracle was done from the grave when his bones resurrected a dead man. God is faithful, none of his word will fall down to the floor. Elisha's double portion had to be fulfilled even after his death. Jesus's words that he spoke in ancient Israel some two thousand years ago are still alive today.

a) Words can build.
b) Words can kill.
c) Words can heal.
d) Words contain faith.
e) Words contain fear.
f) Words can be deployed.
g) Words have authority.
h) Words are creative.
i) Words depict personality.
j) Words can be ignited from hell.
k) Words live after our death.
l) Words penetrate into the spirit realm.
m) Words can bewitch you.
n) Words can bring breakthroughs.
o) Words can usher in a curse or blessing.
p) Words can change your world.

q) Words can invoke the miraculous.
r) Words can design your future.
s) Words can corrupt manners.
t) Words can bring conversion.
u) Words can connect you to God.
v) Words can change us.
w) Words sculpture your atmosphere.
x) Words alter your perception.
y) Words can change your season.
z) Words can shorten your lifespan.

CHAPTER FOURTEEN

DESTINY-MINDED

The high destiny of the individual is to serve rather than to rule. Albert Einstein

Romans 8v29: (For whom he did foreknow, he also did predestinate to be conformed to the image of his Son, that he might be the firstborn among many brethren.)

Where are you going? All people have a destiny but some don't realize it. A sound mind makes a demand on your destiny. The destiny has all that you should become and vision has a way of bringing you to it. The mere thought of a destiny energizes the feeble knees and the drooping hands towards an action plan. Destiny is calling many but only a few take heed of its orders and urgings. The greatest enemy to your destiny is your last success-keep moving. Jesus was seeing the joy that was set before him and he managed to endure the cross. A different management of life's business is introduced when destiny comes into play. Being destiny-minded brings joy in a dark hour and hope in a hopeless time.

Destiny-minded people turn from victims to victors, and from a level of exasperation to exhilaration. Having a vision is like taking a straight line despite the resistance. Visionaries do not follow the path of less resistance but they go against the current. Wandering is reduced or eradicated where there is a vision. Imagine building a sky-scraper without a plan; this is a recipe for disaster. The builder without a plan will forget some components which would force him to destroy a part of the building in order to fit them in. This is retrogressive in terms of time, resources, and progress.

Knowing your destiny will induce and inject direction. There were countless times when Mark Zuckerberg could have made a quick return by selling his corporation to willing buyers. But he believed that the future had tremendous dividends. Mark stuck to the plan. He understood that Rome wasn't built in one day. He continued to create momentum and clung to his vision. Stoicism is a school of the Hellenistic philosophy founded in Athens. Stoicism teaches the development of self-control and fortitude as a means of overcoming destructive emotions. Stoics believed in delayed gratification. The exact opposite group of the Epicureans believed in instant gratification. It pays to be patient.

The one who says that he has arrived when he is still on the way does not know where he is going. If you do not know where you are going any road will take you there. If you do not tell people where you are going they will lead you to their destiny. Many die without accomplishing the minutest part of their vision. Elisha was not moved by Bethel nor Jericho because he had a destiny. He did not worry about the journey-he knew what he wanted. He did not follow when it was convenient but always. Elisha was determined to stay with Elijah as long as he lived and in another portion of scripture "he says as long as the Lord lives". Job says that; 'when I come forth I shall be as pure as gold' because he was seeing his destiny, he knew that the problems were not the end. He also knew that he was not defined by his circumstances. Know who you are, that's what determines your worth-it's not in your possessions. The way you see yourself is the way you perform. You can't get to the top with the mind that is immersed in failure. Confront the weak sides of your mind and work on them. Challenge your mind to the next level. You are loaded but you need to die empty after executing your purpose. Unleash your success. Embrace the change-transition to your destiny. You were not born to fit in but to be distinctive. Destiny-minded people solicit the help of mentors.

Examples of mentorship.
- a) *Ruth's mentor was Naomi.*
- b) *Joshua's mentor was Moses.*
- c) *Timothy's mentor was Paul.*
- d) *Elisha's mentor was Elijah.*
- e) *Esther's mentor was Mordecai.*
- f) *Oprah Winfrey's mentor was Maya Angelou.*
- g) *Albert Einstein's mentor was Max Talmey.*
- h) *Warren Buffet was mentored by Benjamin Graham.*
- i) *Alexander the Great was mentored by Aristotle.*
- j) *Kenneth Copeland was mentored by Oral Roberts.*
- k) *Jerry Savelle was mentored by Kenneth Copeland.*
- l) *Mark Zuckerburg said his inspiring mentor was Steve Jobs.*
- m) *Bill gates credits part of his success to his mentor Warren Buffet.*
- n) *Mark Cuban says that he was mentored by his dad.*

CHAPTER FIFTEEN

BUSINESS-MINDED

There is only one boss. The customer. And he can fire everybody in the company from the chairman on down, simply by spending his money somewhere else. Sam Walton.

Proverbs 22:29 ('Seest thou a man diligent in his business? He will stand before Kings.)

The Bible says "in the beginning was the Word and the Word was with God and the Word was God. The Word was with God in the beginning. Everything came into being through the Word, and without the Word nothing came into being. What came into being through the Word was life, and the life was the light for all people". The Greek meaning for 'word', is logos. Logos means an idea or thought. Everything was created through God's idea. God is the author of ideas. Business is born from ideas, concepts and insights. An idea is defined as a thought, plan, scheme, method and a conception, that potentially resides in the mind as a product of mental activity. An idea is not useful until it's used. Remove your idea from under the bushel. Expose it. Don't take your ideas to the grave. Work on that idea till you realize it. There are a lot of opportunities that we haven't tapped into. Small ideas form small companies. An idea is more important than money. A thought can lead you to the money you need. Upward thoughts lead to an elevated life. Prosperity is not automatic. Automatic means something that is done without the need to do hardly anything to accomplish it. Be strategic about getting to your destiny.

God had thoughts of all the creation. He spoke the creation into being as a projection from his mind. The underlying factorial reason for a business is the making of profits. The moment the decline is experienced, an adjustment of the system is required. Diligence is a prerequisite for success in business. Diligence is steadfast application, assiduousness and industry—the virtue of hard work. We all have negative influences in our lives that threaten our opportunities of being wealthy. Change your views towards money and money will begin to follow your life. Money is not the root of all evil, but the love of it is the root of all evil. Solomon says money answers all things. Change your perception towards money. You can't attract what you detest. Change your perception towards people and they will be attracted to you. They are just your mirror.

Proverbs 12:23:(The hand of the diligent shall bear rule.)

Psalms 1:4: (Whatsoever he does prospers).

Forced labor isn't a sign of diligence because you are not working out of your own volition. Business people are usually former employees who got mad and fed up. There is an anointing for craftsmanship and innovation: (Exodus 36:1). God gives us the power to create wealth. God has all the science, art, intuition, intelligence, gifts, talents, skills, strength, ideas, concepts, instincts and insights that we need for our prosperity. God can make something from nothing and he can hang the worlds on nothing. Joseph was a true businessman because he made profits by exchanging goods and he made Egypt very rich. God has the desire to see us prosper. Jesus spoke 23 out of 37 parables on money.

There are 500 verses on prayer and less than 500 verses on faith but there are 2000 verses on money and possessions.

Business-minded people don't know it all, they seek constructive help to advance in their work. They seize the present opportunity because tomorrow may not have the same openings. A research was carried out and it showed the following about entrepreneurs: 45% had no business plan at all, 25% just had a skeleton plan, 30% wrote up a fully-fledged plan. Successful businesses plan before embarking on any execution and action. Plan your work and work your plan. Success is not a place, but it is a collection of well-planned experiences. Successful businesses have goals. Goals show the thoughts of leaders and hence create it's future. Goals that are clear and achievable have the power to maximize results. Money and profit of any form in business is just a part of the rewards for thinking in categories of specific and precise goals.

Some traits of successful business-people are:
- They associate with faithful people.
- They are after the satisfaction of customers.
- They employ others to complement them.
- They believe in themselves.
- They love details.
- They don't just plan but they act.
- They take risks.
- They have role models.
- They think it through.
- They are relational.
- They do an extra mile.
- They put their mind to it.
- They buy low and sell high.
- They leave a ding on the world.
- They believe in excellence.
- They believe in ownership.

- They are honest.
- They ask meaningful questions.
- They reposition themselves.
- They are dedicated.
- They walk with the wise.
- They are versatile.
- They stick to the plan.
- They exercise.
- They wake up early-Margaret Thatcher would wake up at 5 am daily.
- They meditate.
- They eat healthy.
- They study books.

There are studies showing that 70 % of lottery winners have no money left after 7 years. It's because their minds are not trained at that level. Therefore they lose everything till their wealth equates their mind because as a man thinks so is he. Turn thoughts into revenue. Program yourself by exposing yourself to wise people. Train your mind for ultimate success. Peter Daniels failed in business but he continued to expand his mind by reading thousands of books. Sir Richard Branson suffers from severe dyslexia, but he's come to regard it as his greatest strength. Richard said "if I could read a balance sheet, I couldn't have done anything in life". Sir Richard Branson trained his mind and he is the chairman of more than 400 companies. Your mind determines your wealth. All of us have weaknesses and vulnerabilities but we need to overcome them. Just like the spider it only has 2 body parts, the thorax and the abdomen but it works its way to the palace. Don't wait forever. Start sowing. Rain will catch up with you. Reframe your situations to rise above your challenges. Several times God told Joshua to be courageous about success. Success will not just fall into our laps. Restructure your thinking. I think, therefore I am.

Warren Buffet accepted a job from his mentor without requesting for a pay. He had a quest to succeed like his role model, who was an expert in investing. He had to look for a mentor in investing. You can't learn from someone you resent. Find a model who has succeeded in the area that you desire to prosper in and be discipled by them. Today Warren Buffet is considered the most successful investor of this century. Buffett is the primary shareholder, chairman and CEO of Berkshire Hathaway and has consistently ranked among the world's wealthiest people.

Business people ask the right questions. Jesus the greatest leader ever, asked a lot of questions. If you ask the right questions, life will change. Chris Gardner did not have many positive male role models as a child. His stepfather was physically abusive to his mother. He developed a deep passion for reading and studying, as he became familiar with the works of Martin Luther King, Jr. and others, his world view expanded beyond the average. Chris Gardner became homeless while raising his young son alone after a divorce. The monumental moment in his life happened, after a business sales call to a San Francisco General Hospital, when he encountered an elegantly-dressed man in a red Ferrari. Gardner asked the man about his career. The man told him that he was a stockbroker and, from that moment on, Gardner's career path was decided. Chris pulled himself up from homelessness by holding many jobs over the years. Today Chris Gardner is an American entrepreneur, investor, stockbroker, motivational speaker, author, and philanthropist. He asked the right question. Chris Gardner turned obstacles and opposition into opportunities. Usually motivation comes from a very difficult situation. You are one idea away from your miracle and breakthrough-redeem the time. Successful people buy time by maximizing on it. Time is money. It's a precious commodity. Follow your passion and find your purpose.

Turn your talent and skills into a business. Success is a learnable skill. We learn by failing, just like the way we learnt to walk, talk and run. David trained himself in using the sling and this skill became handy in the face of the giant Goliath. Hone your skills. Get better at what you do.

Everyone is intelligent in their own way. Don't limit yourself to an IQ test. Don't be contained by it. Many millionaires have so-called low IQ results but are successful anyway. Use what God has given you in the form of a gift, ability, capability, capacity and talent. Don't be limited. Some believe in going to school and getting a job and working for the rest of their lives, then retire and die as it were. But the rich people have a different mindset that makes them employers and not employees. A job will pay your bills but can't make you wealthy. Working for a mere paycheck will rob you of the time of thinking about ideas that would make you wealthy. Ideas are like nuggets hidden in deep waters. They need to be drawn but cannot be drawn by tired minds beaten by a day's job. The cycle of hand to mouth creates a state of crisis management. You are just managing a crisis and not having time to shoot off from the mire. Follow your passion and it will make you wealthy. Bill Gates dropped out of Harvard and pursued his instincts and is the richest man in the world. Don't be afraid to risk starting your own business, surprise yourself. A lot of people hesitate to get into business because of a poor self-image, poor self-portrait and they don't believe in themselves well. They doubt their capacity and talk themselves out of every venture. Train your mind to see opportunities that can't be seen by physical eyes. Samson was creative and resourceful, he saw a weapon in the jawbone of an ass and slew an entire army with it, (Judges 15v16).

Successful people do what poor people only talk about. Your life is a printout of your thoughts. You do business according to the level of your conviction ingrained and tattooed in your mind. Busyness can be an enemy to your production and business.

Advantages of starting your own business.

a) You have more time with your family.
b) You can't be fired.
c) You have an opportunity to implement your personal vision.
d) You have more opportunity to create generational wealth.
e) You exercise the power of decision-making.
f) You send a message about the power of your faith.
g) You become more beneficial to your society.
h) You have more control of your future.
i) You have the opportunity to exercise leadership.
j) Your sphere of influence increases.
k) You have opportunity to set standards.
l) You can leave inheritance for your children's children.
m) You can establish God's covenant in the earth.
n) You create long term solutions.
o) You create a life with more options.
p) Your money gets to a level of working for you.

There is a relationship between desire and fulfilment. Be willing and desirous to take a risk in business. Risk has to be managed properly and profits will be gained. Fear eats up our success. These are some of the risks

a) Operational risk-this loss results from a failed process, people, systems or outside circumstances.
b) Compliance risk-this loss results from not following laws, rules, regulations, policies and procedures.
c) Reputational risk-this loss results from negative publicity of the organization conduct and practices. Big organizations have a public relations department that manages their image through media and other avenues.
d) Strategic risk-this loss results from not responding to change on a timely basis. Don't procrastinate. Act today. Be proactive and not reactive. Some business opportunities have an expiry date.

CHAPTER SIXTEEN

GENERATIONAL THINKING

There is nothing I'm any more passionate than empowering the next generation. T. D. Jakes

Proverbs 13v22: (A good man leaveth an inheritance to his children's children: and the wealth of the sinner is laid up for the just.)

Generational thinkers are visionaries. They see beyond themselves. They work for their children's children. Leaving a legacy and an inheritance for the next generation is their mandate. A good man leaves an inheritance for his children's children. He is concerned about three generations. If the average length of one generation is 80 years, then it means three generations are equated to 240 years, this is how far the generational thinkers see. They have a passion to activate the passion of the next generation. Our children should go further than us because they stand on our shoulders. We must plant trees that will give our descendants some fruits. What gifts are we going to give to the next generations? The investments into the posterity and the offspring is invaluable. We have a responsibility to know that more is expected from us.

Work hard, have a vision and take some risks to build generationally. The torch should be passed and not dropped. The Constitution of the United States is the supreme law of the United States of America. This constitution was made with a never-ending generation in mind. We owe it to ourselves and to the next generation to create voices that govern us to generational thinking. Most politicians do not look beyond the next election to the next generation. Lack of generational thinking creates a generational gap that causes tremendous confusion and chaos. We have gained great heritage from the previous and preceding generations and we should do more for the succeeding ones. Our God is generational, and beyond-He is eternal. We must bring up and empower the next generation-this is the greatest legacy.

The things you want in life are always possible and accessible but the process of getting them is not just easy-if it were so, anybody and everybody would get them conveniently. Nothing just happens. Successful people do what unsuccessful people will not do. Greatness does not go on sale, neither is it discounted. The repository of greatness is usually camouflaged in pain. Overcome the pain to unlock the treasure trove.

Generational thinkers have a bigger view of life. They conquer adversity. They don't hold back-they live a full and abundant life. They contribute generously and magnanimously to others, even to the unborn. Purpose is what their lives revolves on. Day and night, they seek to solve problems rather than create them. They focus on seeing the best in everyone because everyone has the potential to change and upgrade. They do daily what others do occasionally because what is done daily becomes dominant and controlling. They don't force other people to fit in a little image, but they have a larger picture which is diverse and accommodating. They wake up early, exercise and work smart. They are radical and go beyond the horizons of their current thought-life. They create more capacity and room.

Generational thinkers don't just give a hand out but a hand up. They are the genesis of succeeding, duplicating, exponential and cumulative success. They are concerned about what will be here a long time after they are gone. The world to come called posterity is always on their minds because they realize that our destinies are tied together. They stand for something and hence they attract both opposition and destiny. They don't wait for someone to do something, they just go ahead and do it. They have a great deposit of ambition and passion which expands opportunities and not contract them, giving the world a sense of vision, hope and future.

Generational thinkers don't waste time, rather they use it effectively. They know and detect time detractors. They are not easily drawn, taken away or diverted from specific goals. They capitalize on their time and it produces for them. They don't just pretend to be busy, but results speak for them. They think about how they can use time better. They don't waste time by blaming others. They understand that learning new and considerable materials is a key element in time management.

Generational thinkers don't just fit in but refuse to be average. They have a higher normal. They believe in launching the next generations by passing the relay baton stick. Generational thinkers exercise divergent and out-of-the-box thinking that brings creativity and innovation. They exceed expectations and go an extra mile. They have superb daily routines that create excellent futures. They make deposits that will upgrade lives. They are pioneers and don't bow down to peer pressure. They are willing to go where others will not go. Generational thinkers believe in cross-pollination-sharing concepts, insights and ideas with others, thereby extending and increasing their capacity to accommodate more in life. Life is larger than one mere individual. There is more to learn from others. Cross-pollination updates the mind and prevents lagging behind.

Summary points
- Generational thinkers are visionaries.
- Leaving a legacy and an inheritance for the next generation is their mandate.
- They have superb daily routines that create excellent futures.

- They don't just pretend to be busy, but results speak for them.
- They don't force other people to fit in a little image, but they have a larger picture which is diverse and accommodating.
- Greatness does not go on sale, neither is it discounted.

CHAPTER SEVENTEEN

THINKING OUTSIDE THE BOX

I like to think outside the box. Look in deeper to what's really going on. I can't stand close minded, shallow people. Unknown.

1 Chronicles 22v7: And David said to Solomon, my son, as for me, it was in my mind to build a house unto the name of the Lord my God

You should have a concept of a life that is outside of your usual perimeters and parameters. If you think at the same level as yesterday, you will get yesterday's results. As we continue to renew our minds the light breaks forth and shines in our lives. The last thing you see before you sleep, works in your mind seven times more than when you are awake. Create a habit of repeating your vision and goals before you go to sleep. See more. Learn to think without blinkers. A clogged mind will produce limited results. King David commanded the strangers in Israel to gather together, and he set stonecutters to hew out stones for the building of the house of God. David prepared iron in abundance and cedar trees without number. David said that the house that was to be built for the Lord was to be exceedingly magnificent, of fame and glory throughout all lands. He therefore made preparation for it lavishly before his death. He called for Solomon his son and charged him to build a house for the

Programming My Mind for Success

Lord, the God of Israel. David said to Solomon, that it was in his heart to build a house to the presence of the Lord his God. But the word of the Lord came to him, saying, "You have shed much blood and have waged great wars; you shall not build a house to My Name, because you have shed much blood on the earth in My sight." David had a mind to build something big for God. Move out of the average conditions of operation. Launch into the deep. David gave generously to God's house. He desired to make it a house of fame.

We look for evidence that reinforces our small models rather than think out of the box. Don't decide to dwell on the comfort zone because it will not challenge the status quo and the usual landscape of your mind. You cannot go back in time and change your dysfunctional background that you grew up under, but you can change the effect it had on your mind. What happens to you is not as important as what happens in your mind. No negative history can stop your success story. Provoke yourself to big thinking. If you can understand everything about your world then it is too small. If you know more than all your peers, then you need to upgrade to other friends who know more than you. Enlarge the horizons and borders. Solicit, summon and invoke new dimensions for your thinking. There are about 86,400 seconds in a day and every second should be translated into an opportunity. What are you doing with your time? Time is precious and needs to be redeemed as chronicled in Ephesians 5:16: (Redeeming *the time, because the days are evil*).

Matthew 5:45: (That ye may be the children of your Father which is in heaven: for he maketh his sun to rise on the evil and on the good, and sendeth rain on the just and on the unjust).

In the above-mentioned verse we learn that God gives us the rain, sunshine, laws and opportunities-we are supposed to take advantage of that. God sends rain and sunshine on the evil and the good people. What we do with this is up to us. Same sun, same rain but different results. No one receives special and sugar-coated rain or sun. The rain doesn't choose certain addresses and zip codes that belong to the just. The response is our responsibility. Laws of nature are given to the just and the unjust-for example the law of seedtime and harvest. Diligent farmers will get a harvest. Also, the opportunity has a lot to play with the above-mentioned story. In the gifts that God gives us, there are hidden opportunities. Opportunities may appear to be opposition, but we should discern. Let's use our minds to exploit the rain, sun, laws and opportunities. Capitalize on the rain, don't wait for golden rain.

People that have low targets will always be victims of the menace of the abortion of their visions. Envisioning the highest and the loftiest is the means for success. The moderate goals will bear little results, but aggressive targets will bring enormous produce. Decide to get tired of subsistence living and enroll for the higher life. Go for it today. The adage of reaching for the sky, allegorically, implies that the sky is rich with stellar objects and anyone can have a great portion of it. It implies vastness. The word "reaching" shows the effort and strategic planning. There is more than you think or imagine in your life. Many successful people have accomplished more in a lifetime than has been accomplished by a hundred men or more put together. Do not be satiated with the surface results but go deeper for more. The difference between a pauper and a billionaire is the way they reach for the sky. One is determined and the other is casual. God wanted to change the reaching and stretching factor of a barren and old couple, therefore God showed Abram the vastness of the stars of the sky and the multiplicity of the sand of the seashore. God blew Abram's mind by telling him that his descendants were going to be as many. God has prepared much more than we are experiencing right now. Stretch. You carry worlds, nations and generations in you. You need to maximize.

Nike allocates about $1,2 billion annually towards the advertising budget so that they can shift people from a certain way of thinking to another. Advertising encourages people to spend impulsively and outside their means. Minds are shifted into another paradigm subliminally. About 100 years ago we had the industrial age, this age was characterized by the need to overcome scarcity of goods. But after world war 2, we had so much products that the businesses had to start advertising to get their goods to be bought. This is the consumer age, where we buy not only what we need but also what we don't need due to the pressure from commercials. Marketers use psychological stratagems and they know that it is possible to change the minds of the people by reciting the same message repeatedly. Repetition is key for mindset change.

Someone said, "and the day came when the risk to remain tight in a bud was more painful than the risk it took to blossom" Eleanor Roosevelt said, "say nothing, do nothing and you will become nothing". Admire someone who is ahead of you. A research showed that people who are friends are usually $2000-$3000 different in their annual salaries because we attract who we are. The law of Averages states that we become an average of the people around us. They receive from us as we receive from them. But we need to intentionally walk with those higher than us. They pull us out of the box and up. Why do you admire those whom you admire? . There should be a reason. Always investigate as to why the great are great. The possibility of moving out of the box increases as you connect to higher minds. You are not wired for inside-of-the-box-thinking but outside-of-the-box-thinking.

We must break the lines that have been drawn around us as limitations and boundaries. Opinions and views of the naysayers can bind us if we let them-be bigger than the average person. Go above and beyond the norm to accomplish the remarkable. There is more to life than you are seeing. Nothing changes till you act. Discover the champion in you. There is an invisible horizon behind the visible horizon. Unload your potential. The Atlantic Ocean is the second-largest of the world's oceanic demarcations. With a total area of about 41 million square miles, it covers approximately 20 % of the Earth's surface. The fish born in the Atlantic Ocean has more exposure and options than that born in a bathtub. Move out into the deeper waters.

Summary points.
- Move out of the average conditions of operation.
- Go above and beyond the norm to accomplish the remarkable.
- We must break the lines that have been drawn around us as limitations
- "Say nothing, do nothing and you will become nothing", Eleanor Roosevelt.
- The law of Averages states that we become an average of the people around us.
- The difference between a pauper and a billionaire is the way they reach for the sky.

CHAPTER EIGHTEEN

A MIND TO WORK

There is no substitute for hard work. Thomas A. Edison

It must be borne in mind that the tragedy of life does not lie in not reaching your goal. The tragedy of life lies in having no goal to reach. Benjamin E. Mays

Nehemiah 2v5 :(And I said unto the king, if it please the king, and if thy servant have found favor in thy sight, that thou wouldest send me unto Judah, unto the city of my fathers' sepulchres, that I may build it).

Nehemiah is the main character of the book of Nehemiah. He is known for rebuilding Jerusalem. Nehemiah was the cupbearer to the king Artaxerxes of Persia. After he heard that the walls of Jerusalem were broken down, he asked for permission to go back and rebuild them. As he was building he faced great opposition from the Samaritans, Ammonites, Philistines and Arabs. Nehemiah as a visionary built the walls in a record-breaking time of 52 days because the people had a mind to work.

Nehemiah 4v6: (So built we the wall; and all the wall was joined together unto the half thereof: for the people had a mind to work).

The team that was being led by Nehemiah had a mind to work and they defied all opposition. Detractors and critics will always be there but keep the main thing as the main thing. Sanballat heard about the building of the walls and he took great indignation and mocked the builders but they stuck to the plan. Tobiah the Ammonite also scorned the Jews but it all came to nothing. There is always contradiction and opposition to our work but fight against the odds. All the builders had a sword girded by their sides as they built. The bad times will launch you into the good times if you persist to have a mind to work. Nothing of value will come to us without real work and perseverence. Plans are only good intentions unless they are implemented. Work is the key to responsibility. Meaningful work brings results in life. Nothing works till you work.

Genesis 2v15: (And the Lord God took the man, and put him into the Garden of Eden to dress it and to keep it).

Adam was given work to tend the garden before the fall, so work is not a curse. He was supposed to dress and tend it. Dreams are never realized without conscientious hard work. Somebody said, "formula for success is: rise early, work hard and strike oil". In all you do, do it well. Make up your mind as to what you need to accomplish, work at it and success will follow. The price of work must be paid in exchange for remunerations. Success is not an accident but an intentional decision to work. Thomas Edison worked late into the nights on the electric light until he reached his programmatic goal. Do what you love and love what you do, and you will never work another day in your life-make work pleasurable. When work is a pleasure, life is immeasurably pleasurable. Most people are always looking forward to the weekend because they hate what they do at their workplaces during the weekdays. Most indulge in glamour at the expense of work and they lose. A sense of urgency and a sense of timing are prerequisites for working to get optimum dividends in any enterprise or business. Put your mind to it wholly and you will achieve your

Programming My Mind for Success

desires. Making up your mind is pivotal in decision-making and working. Getting things done without demanding recognition is the highest level of service. A mind set to work deals with targets and meets deadlines. Never hope more than you work.

Genesis 37v14: (And he said to him, Go, I pray thee, see whether it be well with thy brethren, and well with the flocks; and bring me word again. So, he sent him out of the vale of Hebron, and he came to Shechem.)

Joseph was sent to look for his brothers and he walked for a long distance on foot in search for his brothers. History has it that he walked for many miles from Hebron to Schechem but he did not find them there, so he walked further to Dothan. This gives us a clue that Joseph was not lazy. A chain of success that is not earned will destroy because earning is a process connected to learning, and learning brings discipline hence university studies are called disciplines. The singular common thread in visionaries is diligence. Visionaries are enterprising and industrious. Romans 12:11, tells us not to be slothful. Even in the house of Potiphar, Joseph became the lead-person over many servants due to diligence. The house of Potiphar had stables, rooms for chariots, servant's quarters, granaries, courtyards, grain bins and many extra rooms. He literally ran a business.

The diligent will rule and lead. There is a big debate of whether leaders are born or made, but I think that both the made or born need grooming, training, apprenticeship and shaping. The making of a leader takes much in terms of preparation and true preparation is much work. Many aspire to be great but aspirations without perspiration is a waste. There are three kinds of people, firstly those who watch others, secondly those who just articulate, and thirdly those that do. Migrate from the wishing level to the practicing level. A story is told of Abraham Lincoln that at ten years of age he decided that he was going to become the President, 'I will prepare and become the President when time is due'. The parents of Moses, Jochebed, and Amram, were diligent in the making of the ark after the Pharaoh had issued an edict that all the male children should die. The ark had bitumen for waterproofing the material on the outside, the inside was made of smooth clay for comfort. This ark was placed by the bulrushes to prevent crocodiles from coming near it and it was strategically positioned at a place of bathing of the Pharaoh's daughter. The sister of Moses, Miriam had to wait for the Pharaoh's daughter and ask for a job offer after the princess had seen the baby. The baby was preserved by God, but the parents cooperated with God. The human heart beats about 115,000 times a day-that's hard work; the organs of the body work hard and I guess we should also.

Ecclesiastes 9:10: 'Whatever your hand findeth to do, do it with all your might'.

Our God does not sleep nor slumber: (Psalms 121:3). In the book of Genesis, God did not rest on the seventh day due to tiredness; but the rest in this case has a sense of pausing to admire and feel the satisfaction for a work well done in the creation of the world. God is diligent. Most gifted people don't like to work, so they end up being credited to nothing. You learn to work by actually working. There is an adage that says, "genius is 99 % perspiration and 1% inspiration".

The Pareto principle also called the 80/20 rule states that an average of 20 % of the organization produces 80 % of the results. This law of the vital few shows that most people don't have a great work ethic. Research shows that on an average 50 % of the time is wasted by an employee on things that have nothing to do with their work. Learning how to focus on work is actually a discipline needed for success in everyday life.

Summary Points.
- Make up your mind as to what you need to accomplish, work at it and success will follow.

- The Pareto principle also called the 80/20 rule states that an average of 20 % of the organization produces 80 % of the results.
- Success is not an accident but an intentional decision to work.
- You learn to work by working.
- Many aspire to be great but aspirations without perspiration is a waste.
- Getting things done without demanding recognition is the highest level of service.

CHAPTER NINETEEN

THE PROGRESSIVE MIND

Without continual growth and progress, such words as improvement, achievement, and success have no meaning. Benjamin Franklin

Genesis 41v43: (And he made him to ride in the second chariot which he had; and they cried before him, Bow the knee: and he made him ruler over all the land of Egypt.)

Joseph's dreams brought him into captivity ultimately, but he didn't stop interpreting dreams. The king of Egypt was in desperate need of an interpretation of his dreams and by divine and timely intervention, Joseph was called to that task when all the magicians and the soothsayers had failed. Joseph was helped by the person he had helped, good works sown will always bring a harvest of great rewards according to Galatians 6v6. The way of a progressive mind is always up and forward. God will elevate you to higher levels beyond the wildest expectations as seen in Ephesians 3v20. As the adage goes, 'from the prison to the palace', Joseph was promoted. He was promoted because he was not stuck in the agony brought by his dreams. He moved forward.

The result after all the hell, turmoil, and chaos was the palace. Your palace will not be destroyed by the problem without your permission. Within a short period of time after the interpretation of the dream, Joseph was put in charge of the complete land of Egypt, he was given a signet ring from the Pharaoh's hand, and he was dressed in fine linen. The gold chain was put around his neck and he was made to ride in a chariot as men shouted in celebration :(Genesis 41v41-43). Joseph was 30 years old when this escalation came into his life, his vision spoke. The vision was fully-grown, and it manifested.

Joseph had a virtuous and progressive mind. He built himself up on pure thoughts. He didn't allow the situations to embitter his life. He kept thinking about good things even in the worst of times. He concentrated his thoughts on his God-given dream. Don't be twisted by the pits, prisons, hatred, anger that we meet in life. The means can engulf us and automatically destroy our end. Thoughts come uninvited, but you can choose as to which thoughts can reside in your mind. When it's important it's not an option-it's a must to choose your thoughts. Every choice has an outcome. A true choice is accompanied by an action. Choose to study the following: good books, good friends and to be a companion of the wise to advance your mind forward.

The weak mindset will produce a weak lifestyle. A different mindset will earn the difference. Change according to the degree of the difference you want to see. A wasted day will produce a broken tomorrow. We lose the future by being stuck in the mud of the past. Looking and sliding backwards leads to perdition. Keep your hands on the plough and go forward. Don't wait for life to happen-make it happen. Nothing just happens. Be willing to go to the next level. Stop the excuses. You can wallow in the quagmire forever unless you interrupt the cycle. Before you quit, try.

We don't choose what happens to us, but we can choose what happens in us and thereby affect the outside eventually. Noble thoughts give concrete and definite form to a successful lifestyle. Sickly thoughts produce a sickly life. Thoughts that enter and control your mind will eventually control your life. Lack of purposeful thoughts will lead to aimlessness. Thoughts of fear lead to massive failure. Be responsible for your thoughts-have a sense of ownership. Deal with your mind. If you take responsibility, it helps you to confront your mistakes. Correct them, map a way forward and move on. Blaming others and circumstances will not produce results but more anger and less control over your life. Two people can be exposed to the same opportunities and still come up with different results. Don't let this world squeeze you into its mold and shape. Thoughts will always seek an expression either in word or deed. The body is moldable and follows the dictates of your thoughts. In 1 Corinthians 9v27, Paul says "I pommel my body". Thoughts are a spring of life. The inner world of our minds can influence the outer world.

2 Kings 5v11: But Naaman was wroth, and went away, and said, Behold, I thought, He will surely come out to me, and stand, and call on the name of the LORD his God, and strike his hand over the place, and recover the leper.

Naaman was the commander of the Syrian army. The LORD had helped him and his troops to defeat many enemies. Naaman was a brave soldier, but he had leprosy. One day while the Syrian troops were raiding Israel, they captured a girl, and she became a servant of Naaman's wife. Sometime later the girl said, "If your husband Naaman would go to the prophet in Samaria, he would be cured of his leprosy." Therefore Naaman left with his horses and chariots and stopped at the door of Elisha's house. Elisha sent someone outside to say to him, "Go wash seven times in the Jordan River. Then you'll be completely cured." But Naaman stormed off, grumbling, "Why couldn't he come out and talk to me? I thought for sure he would stand in front of me and pray to the LORD his God, then wave his hand over my skin and cure me. His servants went over to him and said, "Sir, if the prophet had told you to do something difficult, you would have done it. So why don't you do what he said? Go wash and be cured." Naaman walked down to the Jordan; he waded out into the water and stooped down in it seven times, just as Elisha had told him. Right away, he was cured, and his skin became as smooth as a child's.

Naaman could not proceed to his healing because of preconceptions. He had an opinion or conception formed in advance from inadequate knowledge or experience, it was just a prejudice and a bias. Naaman had an idea or opinion formed beforehand. His preconception gave him an assumption and a negative image that was going to hinder his healing and miracle. Preconceptions can instigate arguments and unnecessary fights. His preconceptions created his presuppositions. When he changed his mind, he received his healing immediately. Speculation can delay, impede, or prevent our miracles. Preconceptions made him prideful and angry. Finally, he took great advise that made him to move forward by changing his thoughts. Thoughts stood in the way of his miracle. Naaman had created a pattern in his mind of how God was to heal him. He was not ready to receive new instructions because of the old tabulated form of methods in his thinking. A bad attitude can delay our miracles and make the process longer. Approach challenges with a great attitude and it will make us to grow. Condemnation, shame and guilt can hinder your progression in God. Don't let preconceptions hinder your purpose.

Discover your purpose in life and bring all your energies to accomplishing it. There is treasure hidden within us that should be released. We are a concentration of riches. Rich in ideas, visions, dreams and concepts. We should discharge what lies dormant in us. Our present success should not retard our motion to the next level of success. God has more for us and he is ready to do more than we can ask nor think. God has set an end for you and you must walk into it. He predestined you-he works the beginning from the end. Destiny keeps our lives on the progressive track. Develop and condition your mindset that this is your opportune time and excellent things are supposed to happen to you. You are the only one keeping yourself back.

Genesis 19:26, (But his wife looked back from behind him, and she became a pillar of salt).

Luke 9:62, (And Jesus said unto him, no man, having put his hand to the plough, and looking back, is fit for the kingdom of God).

Exodus 13:17, (And it came to pass, when Pharaoh had let the people go, that God led them not through the way of the land of the Philistines, although that was near; for God said, Lest peradventure the people repent when they see war, and they return to Egypt).

Progressive people don't entertain going backwards. Shrinking is to draw back and instinctively it makes us unprofitable. In accounting terms, shrinkage is the loss between the manufacturing of a product to the point of sale. Shrinkage results in loss of profits. Let us not contract and abbreviate the length and breadth of the vision. We should not live below the standard. Apathy precedes a collapse. We should stop the downward spiral. Going backwards leads to destruction and perdition. Lot's wife looked back, and she became a pillar of salt. A man who puts his hands to the plough and looks back is unfit for the kingdom business. Israel was taken through a longer way to Canaan, because the shorter one had some enemies. God knew that the enemies would fight against Israel and change their minds from going to Canaan. A resolute mind does not turn back but goes forward. Going backwards takes us the longer way. God said to Joshua that his servant Moses was dead and that he was supposed to lead Israel across the Jordan River into the land that he was giving to them. You can't grieve forever. It's time for a takeover. Time to cross the Jordan into Canaan. It's not what they say to you but what you say to yourself that matters. You have it in you to relocate in your mind.

A human grows from a cell, to an embryo, to a fetus, to an infant, to an adolescent, to an adult, until he is elderly. There is a progression. It is not easy to grow out of something. People trying to stop an addiction usually have withdrawal symptoms. Overcome the symptoms. Desire is a pre-requisite for growth. People love inertia or the tendency to stay in one place unless interrupted by an external force. Progress is accomplished by daring and acting. Giving excuses and only cheering the success of others will erase the mind for us to go forward-we need balance. For us to grow we have to see the solutions and not only the problems. A twisted self-image is usually born from rejection, agony, anger and trauma. Rejected people have a propensity to reject themselves. Fear of rejection brings stagnancy-we are hesitant to try anything. People with rejection don't build strong relationships because they are afraid of being rejected. A mind contained by failure will not allow growth. Don't complicate the simple things in life. Simplicity is crucial for success. You will never succeed if you hold on to past issues, these will eat up your strength. Forget the past, reach out to the future and keep pressing. Surround yourself with optimistic people that will be a conducive environment for your progress. God cannot be limited or formatted to a certain way and method of doing things. He is the God of all flesh and can do anything at any time for anybody. He is sovereign. He reigns over all.

Summary points
- The way of a progressive mind is always up and forward.
- Surround yourself with optimistic people that will be a conducive environment for your progress.
- Don't complicate the simple things in life.
- A twisted self-image is usually born from rejection.
- Progress is accomplished by daring and taking action.
- A bad attitude can delay our miracles and make the process longer.

CHAPTER TWENTY

GRASSHOPPER MENTALITY

When I started my last business, I didn't receive a paycheck for 13 months. The average person can't handle that pressure. Robert Kiyosaki

Numbers 13v27-30:(²⁷ *And they told him, and said, We came unto the land whither thou sentest us, and surely it floweth with milk and honey; and this is the fruit of it.* ²⁸ *Nevertheless the people be strong that dwell in the land, and the cities are walled, and very great: and moreover, we saw the children of Anak there.* ²⁹ *The Amalekites dwell in the land of the south: and the Hittites, and the Jebusites, and the Amorites, dwell in the mountains: and the Canaanites dwell by the sea, and by the coast of Jordan.* ³⁰ *And Caleb stilled the people before Moses, and said, let us go up at once, and possess it; for we are well able to overcome it.)*

The twelve spies were sent to spy out the land and bring back a report. The ten spies concentrated on the grapes, giants and grasshoppers but Caleb and Joshua focused on God's ability. Caleb said let's go up at once because he didn't want to convince himself out of God's will by adhering to the evil report. Don't talk yourself out of your dream. The ten had a negative and grasshopper mentality-they had self-imposed limitations. The grasshopper image was tattooed on their minds. Nobody called them grasshoppers, but they did it by themselves. They saw themselves in their mind as grasshoppers. The inferiority complex made them to see less of themselves. A grasshopper image will produce grasshopper deeds and life. The ten saw themselves as nothing. They had a poor sense of value about themselves. They belittled themselves. No one can bring you down without your permission, you are the problem if you permit your fall. What are you saying about yourself? The giants did not tell them that they were like grasshoppers, but they saw it in their own minds. They had a wrong picture about themselves in their minds. Grasshoppers don't occupy their possessions and their land. How you see yourself in your mind matters a lot. How you see yourself determines how people see you. What you focus on longest becomes the strongest. Give yourself some credit. You are not a grasshopper. The ten spies didn't believe in themselves. The spies had the opportunity to create their own paths. They exposed themselves to wrong messages instead of God's message. They saw themselves as grasshoppers and became and behaved like them. The ten spies cut themselves short by their wrong thinking. They had inferiority complex. They believed in the power of their history of slavery than in God's power of total deliverance. Don't let your negative history erase your positive future. Dare to see more about you. If God be for you, who can be against you. You are more than a conqueror. You are unique and valiant. Seeing ourselves as grasshoppers is a distrust of God's faith in us. It is an erroneous sense of value of God's masterpiece. You are his priciest masterpiece. You are fearfully and wonderfully made.

    Caleb and Joshua were the minority but were ready to face rejection for what they believed, and they positioned themselves to deal with the state of discomfort, but discomfort propelled them to the next level. They were prepared to override the words of the naysayers. Thoughts bear fruits, the ten spies died in the wilderness, but Caleb and Joshua occupied the promise land. Their thoughts carried them to Canaan. Their thoughts produced their destiny. Their minds shaped their beliefs and their beliefs shaped their lives.

Right believing produces right living. Right believing leads to the right destiny. Caleb and Joshua took a risk. A risk is inherently connected to rewards. They were ready to be courageous and to be ridiculed at the same time. They lived by design and not by default. Negative thoughts continue to thrive automatically until they are stopped intentionally by you. Greatness lies dormant and latent in you till it is aroused.

Achievement is a thought-style before it is a lifestyle. We all have a thought process or a thought pattern that can be altered and adjusted. Upgrade and update your thinking. Thinking has a pattern or a design. Some designs in our minds lead to self-destruction. God wanted Gideon to change his mind, so he could operate from a position of strength rather than that of weakness. Others will try to limit you but that should not stop you. Stay encouraged. The belief in yourself is more important and vital than what anyone else thinks nor believes.

Concentrate on the dream. The ten spies brought forth an evil report, that is an unauthorized, partial and distorted truth which influenced them to form a negative opinion about a certain situation or person. A good report brings the world, the family and circumstances into the right perspective. The evil report spread among Israel and Israel was disheartened. Fear spread and molded the thinking of a nation. The whole generation was infected by the negative report of ten men. Ten men with an evil report killed a whole nation. Fear led to death in the wilderness. Irrigate your mind and life with optimism by hanging around the positive company. Optimistic people see an opportunity in every difficult situation.

Be careful of your relationships. They rub off on you subliminally. Have people around you that you want to be like. Change your circle and your circumstances will change. Apostle Paul encourages us to mark those that cause division and contention. Fear is contagious. Fear can impede the display of your greatness. There is greatness in you.

Israel always complained and murmured. When they complained, it pulled them backwards rather than forward. Complaining is a definition for denouncing God. Israel was punished for it and they could not reach Canaan, their destiny. They made permanent decisions based on a temporary and momentary situation and could not delay their gratification. Israel didn't have an ownership mentality. God had plans to bring them to great houses that they had not built but they died in the wilderness due to bad thoughts housed in their minds. God delivered them from Egypt, but they resisted deliverance from their oppressed mindsets.

You can think and speak all the way to your death. The journey took the Israelites forty years instead of eleven days. Doubt creates resistance for our progress. Israel was in slavery for more than four centuries. They became conditioned to being slaves and servants and could not easily change from that. Slavery was a norm for them. They could not think at a higher level of success. Success was out of their circle of thinking. They were trained to be under a taskmaster. Taskmasters made decisions for them and they just followed instructions. Being on their own without their taskmasters was very strange for them. Their mentality made them victims instead of victors. They changed their topography on the outside but that did not alter their thinking-their thinking was stuck in a place called Egypt. The attachment to Egypt was more than in the physical realm alone, it was also in the mental realm. The pressure from the slavery warped their thinking. They acquired a twisted, corrupted, brutalized, deformed and a tortured thinking that had the capacity to obstruct them from prosperity. Out of slavery but still functioning with an enslaved mind. Out of Egypt but stuck to the mode of operation of Egypt. An enslaved mind brings wandering and lack of movement and growth. Israel's minds could not contain and receive the promise that God had for them. We should not be stuck in a place in our minds at the expense of progression and change. Israel became pessimistic because they saw a difficulty in every opportunity.

As the adage goes, they were out of Egypt, but Egypt was still within them. Israel could not change their minds in forty years and they died. They permitted slavery to determine their destiny. Their obsession of Egypt frustrated their reach for Canaan. Their taskmasters were not present physically, but they were present mentally. The ten spies are a true sample of the whole nation of Israel. They had a sub-conscious of inferiority complex passed from generation to generation over the four hundred years of exploitation. They didn't have a good self-image, it had been damaged. They were framed by a slave's mentality. They would quickly get discouraged despite of the wondrous things that God was doing among them. Insecurity ruled supreme. Anxiety was ingrained in their thought patterns. They were suspicious hence they doubted God and did not believe God's prophet, Moses.

Miracles could not change their minds. They saw the parting of the Red sea, they were led by a cloud by day, led by a pillar of fire by night, they received manna and got water from the rock. God had sworn to lead them into the promise land, but their minds shortchanged all that. The solemn declaration, promise and invoking by God was resisted by the minds of Israel. God did not force them. Their minds could not contain the new substance that God had for them. They died in a place away from destiny because their minds were retrogressive. Israel memorialized the past hurts, and slavery- this pulled them back. 1 Chronicles 4v9: "And his mother called his name Jabez, which means pain". According to, 1 Samuel 4v21: "And She named the child Ichabod, which means the glory has departed". Don't memorialize and build a monument of your pain, sadness and failure. Weeping may endure for a night, but joy comes in the morning. It's time to rejoice. The Glory is back !.

Israel always blamed Moses for no apparent reason. They told him that he was responsible for their death in the wilderness. They would always find a reason to see a problem where there was no problem at all. Their minds were enslaved and trained to wallow in misery. Don't blame the past, present or others for the situation you are in now-take responsibility. Respond with ability. Blaming others is a way of wanting to deflect our inadequacies onto others. It reduces your confrontation against what is bringing you down. When you complain, you expend your energy on nothing and hence no solutions are found from that at all. By complaining you create a mirage of thinking that you have done something when you haven't in real sense.

A mirage is an optical effect that is sometimes seen at sea, in the desert, or over a hot pavement, that may have the appearance of a pool of water or a mirror in which distant objects are seen inverted. Complaining is an inability to respond properly to issues. Such acts condition you to run away from challenges. Challenges are a doorway to promotion and success. Never be glad about a life without challenges and results.

Concentrating on others at your expense reduces time to discover your value, potential and identity. Don't waste time. Deal with it. Wasting time disturbs the flow of a lifetime. The way you use time will determine what becomes of you. Time is vital because it is the substratum of life. Israel was ready to go back to Egypt. God has no pleasure in those who have a desire to go back. Faith leads us forward and upward. They could not focus on Canaan. Deliverance from Egypt is not a guarantee of the deliverance of our minds. But it is possible to have our minds changed. God gave Israel a promise because he knew they had the ability to receive it, but they resisted the Holy one.

Summary Points.
- The way you use time will determine what becomes of you.
- Concentrating on others at your expense reduces time to discover your value, potential, treasure and identity.

- Never be glad about a life without challenges and results.
- Complaining is an inability and failure to respond to issues properly.
- Blaming others is a way of wanting to deflect our inadequacies onto others.
- Don't permit slavery of the mind to determine and predicate your destiny.

CHAPTER TWENTY ONE

PROGRAMMING THE MIND

The secret of living a life of excellence is merely a matter of thinking thoughts of excellence. Really, it's a matter of programming our minds with the kind of information that will set us free. Charles R. Swindoll

Ephesians 4v23: (And be renewed in the spirit of your mind;)

Colossians 2v14: (Blotting out the handwriting of ordinances that was against us, which was contrary to us, and took it out of the way, nailing it to his cross;)

Our lives are built around beliefs, be careful of what kind of belief you carry. A belief based on misinformation will make us to miss a lot in life. A life based on a dysfunctional belief will cause us to malfunction. We need to pull down this community of wrong thoughts. Replace them with the right thoughts. We were programmed by our environment and genetics. Teachers, parents, siblings, friends, workmates, employers; all these contributed to the programming. Unfortunately most of the programming was negative, hence we have a propensity and tendency to be negative. We naturally gravitate towards the bad. Scripts are written commands, prescriptions or sentences. There are scripts in our minds that are controlling us daily. But we need another scripting from the scriptures. The mind doesn't like new instructions, it would rather relax with the old comfort zone.

Joseph had some dreams at an early age but when he told his brothers and parents-he received opposition against what the God-given dreams had programmed in him. Joseph wasn't deprogrammed by the situations that he went through. He didn't drop his allegiance to his vision. Satisfaction eats away our passion. Joseph wasn't satisfied by the stops along the way till he reached the end. Joseph was surrounded by doubters but he endured. God doesn't tell you to leave Egypt without a Canaan. They had to leave an Egyptian mentality and replace it with a Promise-land mentality. They had to leave the scarcity mentality and get an abundance mentality. Replace negative thoughts with the positive. Your thoughts determine your plans. They dictate your future. They predict your harm or hope. If you focus on positive thoughts you will amount to something great.

Genesis 13v14-15: (And the LORD *said unto Abram, after that Lot was separated from him, Lift up now thine eyes, and look from the place where thou art northward, and southward, and eastward, and westward: For all the land which thou seest, to thee will I give it, and to thy seed forever.)*

And there was a strife between the herdsmen of Abram's cattle and the herdsmen of Lot's cattle. And Abram said unto Lot, Let there be no strife between me and thee. Is not the whole land before you? separate yourself from me, if you will take the left hand, then I will go to the right; or if you depart to the right hand, then I will go to the left. Lot chose the land first. The Lord said to Abram to lift up his eyes and look from the place where he was, northward, southward, eastward and westward. For all the land that he saw the Lord promised it to him and his posterity forever. All that land that he saw was the measure of his inheritance. If he saw a vast expanse of land that would belong to him. We program our minds by seeing what we must possesses. We need to have pictures of the things we are desiring before us. Abram saw what he was going to inherit and receive. See pictures of God's promises.

Luke 4v13:(And when the devil had ended all the temptation, he departed from him for a season.)

The devil attacks us in the mind until we reach a point of psychological exhaustion-this is when you begin to believe in his tricks and wiles. He tempted Jesus but Jesus fought back with the word of God. The devil left him until another favorable or opportune time. The devil keeps fighting and coming back. When we don't fight back, the devil's lies will cause instability till we fall. Adam and Eve succumbed to the devils tricks because they didn't use the word that God gave to them. When Adam sinned we all sinned because we were in him. But through Christ the whole humankind was made alive and saved.

If you don't program your mind with the word, anybody else or anything will. No one can impose their thoughts on you without your permission. We program our minds by what we see, hear and understand. Hollywood is controlling how we think and perceive life through their products and programs. They are shaping our value systems at a global level. The movies have a process of making us to adapt, imitate values with the intent to deceive. Who is controlling your psychological processes? The controllers of your mind will give you a lack of self-worth, a doubt and uncertainty, and a feeling of not measuring up to society's standards. Those who control your mind will control your outcome. The outside can occupy, colonize and dominate your mind if you permit it. We should be careful of how we consider and regard things in our minds because a course of action is built from them. A balance or a state of equilibrium in the mind is required to upgrade in life. Don't think of yourself more highly or lowly than you ought. We need to harness and restrain our minds. There are forces that will throw negative ideas but we should fight against them.

The world is promoting and defending evil habits and thoughts through music, art and drama. They sponsor activities, books and movies which distort and pollute our minds. Mental pollution is the introduction of contaminants into the environment of our minds that cause adverse changes. You have control over what comes into your mind-don't relinquish your keys to the world. Your thoughts will generate, produce and birth your actions. To regulate our actions, we need to check the thoughts in our minds. Don't incubate or promote the embryonic development of wrong thoughts and desires.

Romans 4v19: And being not weak in faith, he considered not his own body now dead, when he was about an hundred years old, neither yet the deadness of Sarah's womb:

Abraham did not consider the deadness of Sarah's womb or his own body now dead. He did not think or meditate about the deadness because that would nullify his faith. Considering is thinking carefully about something with an intent to take action. Don't turn over in your mind or ponder on thoughts that are against God's will. Don't take into account words, situations and thoughts that bring doubt and unbelief. The devil wants you to build your life around your mistakes and failures. He gives you a bad name and a stigma. Modification of your mind around your negative image is his specialization.

Exodus 1v13: And the Egyptians made the children of Israel to serve with rigor:

Conditioning is the learning process by which the behavior of an organism becomes dependent on an event occurring in its environment. The Israelites were conditioned and programmed through slavery for 430 years. They served with rigor and they were afflicted. Their thoughts aborted God's promises. Their thoughts led them to destruction. Their thoughts diverted them from the promiseland. Slavery reinforced self-hatred, emotional trauma, psychological trauma, servitude, wrong identity and lack of confidence. Slavery deprived them of trust. They could not even trust the living God who delivered them from the hand of Pharaoh. They were treated as personal property, they worked against their wills, they were vulnerable to extreme violence and they worked like animals. The promise was ready for them but they were not ready for it. The devil targets our minds and brings suggestions to create doubt of God's word.

Exodus 2v23:And it came to pass in process of time, that the king of Egypt died: and the children of Israel sighed by reason of the bondage, and they cried, and their cry came up unto God by reason of the bondage.

Exodus 16v3:And the children of Israel said unto them, Would to God we had died by the hand of the Lord in the land of Egypt, when we sat by the flesh pots, and when we did eat bread to the full; for ye have brought us forth into this wilderness, to kill this whole assembly with hunger.

In the above-referenced verses, we see a contradiction. In the former verse they cried and sighed by reason of the bondage, but in the latter verse they are crying to literally go back into slavery. They remembered the bread and flesh pots of Egypt. They were doubleminded. Torn between two opinions. They could not appreciate where they were going because their minds were in the past. There is no progress in double-mindedness. They accused Moses of wanting to kill them in the wilderness. Moses as their deliverer had their interests at heart but they could not see that at all. They turned aside quickly out of the way which God commanded them and they tempted him. Israel was stiff-necked. Their mentality hindered them from their destiny. Israel had a mindset that promoted Pharaoh's system as compared to God's system. They forgot that they were God's special people and not Pharaoh's people. We cannot be successful if our minds are against the mind of God. The mind and will of God is his word.

The conversation that you usually have with yourself is the conversation that you extend to others. Contrary internal conversations should be eradicated. The ten spies had a negative internal conversation that made them ultimately to disbelieve God. In the bible, there was a woman who had been bleeding for twelve years. She had gone to many doctors, and they had not done anything except cause her a lot of pain. She had paid them all the money she had. But instead of getting better, she only got worse. The woman had heard about Jesus, so she came up behind him in the crowd and barely touched his clothes. She had said to herself, "If I can just touch his clothes, I will get well." As soon as she touched them, her bleeding stopped, and she knew she was well. At that moment Jesus felt power go out from him. He turned to the crowd and asked, "Who touched my clothes?" His disciples said to him, "Look at all these people crowding around you! How can you ask who touched you?" But Jesus turned to see who had touched him. The woman knew what had happened to her. She came shaking with fear and knelt down in front of Jesus. Then she told him the whole story. Jesus said to the woman, "You are now well because of your faith. May God give you peace! You are healed, and you will no longer be in pain." She had a positive internal conversation, "She had said to herself, "If I can just touch his clothes, I will get well". Negative internal conversation can impede your healing and miracles.

Summary points
- A belief based on misinformation will make you miss a lot in life.
- A life based on a dysfunctional belief will cause you to malfunction.
- We need to pull down the community of wrong thoughts.
- There are scripts in our minds that are controlling us daily.

- Mental pollution is the introduction of contaminants into the environment of our minds.
- The conversation that you usually have with yourself is the conversation that you extend to others.

CHAPTER TWENTY TWO

THINK ON PURPOSE

All successful people, men and women are big dreamers. They imagine what their future could be, ideal in every respect, and then they work every day toward their distant vision, that goal or purpose. Brian Tracy

Philippians 4v8 (Finally, brethren, whatsoever things are true, whatsoever things are honest, whatsoever things are just, whatsoever things are pure, whatsoever things are lovely, whatsoever things are of good report; if there be any virtue, and if there be any praise, think on these things.)

Think purposeful thoughts on purpose. We become like the repeated pattern of the thoughts in our minds. Thinking on purpose creates a deep narrative structure in us that produces deliverables. Almost 90 % of all sicknesses are connected to wrong thinking. You become what you focus on. You don't get in life what you want or need but you get what you are-so think well because you are what you think. Your thoughts determine the color or condition of your mind. Don't put poison in your mind. Rain is liquid water in the form of droplets that has condensed from atmospheric water vapor and then precipitated—that is, become heavy enough to fall under gravity. Thoughts gathered over a long time become heavy like rain and start to manifest. We need to gather the right thoughts so that when we realize them, they will be profitable and beneficial.

Become deliberate and intentional about your thoughts. Fix your thoughts on good things. Shift your thoughts away from the bad things. Weigh and take account of these things. Fix your mind on helping people, serving them and worshipping God. Cogitate on useful and profitable thoughts.

Thoughts of fidelity, progressive ideas, escalating concepts, elevating plans and love are worthy. Recite, rehearse and think on scriptures deliberately. Think rightly and you will succeed. Don't worry about money but focus your thoughts on purpose and the money will follow. Think of winning, accomplishing what you were born for. Set your thoughts just like you set the alarm clock or the thermostat. Remote controls are devices used to issue commands from a distance to televisions or other consumer electronics such as DVD players, stereo systems and dimmers. Remote controls for these devices are usually small wireless handheld objects with an array of buttons for adjusting various settings such as television channels, track numbers, and volume. In the same vein we should issue commands to our minds derived from the word of God. We need to adjust our mind's settings by the Bible. The Bible is the best-seller in the whole world, about five billion copies sold so far. It has 31173 verses and 1189 chapters. It was written by 40 different authors over a period of 1500 years. You cannot expect to break the present limitations until you change your thinking. Thinking on pure thoughts has proved to decrease stress and risk of coronary artery disease. It also improves, resistance to catching the common cold, health, breathing, a better sense of well-being and reduces the risk of pregnant women. Love thinks of no evil. Love keeps no record of wrong.

Mathew 6v31: Therefore take no thought, saying, What shall we eat? or, What shall we drink? or, Wherewithal shall we be clothed?

Here the scriptures show us that thoughts are linked to our words. Don't take thoughts that bring words of doubt. Don't confess shortage. We should not worry about life, drinks, food, clothes but we are to consider the fowls of the air that don't sow nor reap. God feeds the fowls of the air sufficiently. Our thoughts should be of provision and supply from God. Thoughts of abundance and not shortage. Worry should not occupy and dominate our thought-life. We are edified to believe God. Worry cannot add anything good except to subtract from it. The mind should not run wild by worrying about tomorrow because God will provide. Worry brings a perpetual uneasiness and anxiety. Your heavenly Father knows well what you need. So do not worry or be anxious about tomorrow, for tomorrow will have worries and anxieties of its own. Sufficient for each day is its own trouble. Worry is like a rocking chair that takes you nowhere. Jesus came to give us abundant life-that is our keynote, fundamental and central message. The devil persuades us to believe otherwise. Believing the devil aborts the currents of favor towards us. You are a summation of the ideas you have chosen to think and believe. Choose life.

Psalm 19v1: (The heavens declare the glory of God; and the firmament sheweth his handywork.)

The heavens formally announce the honor of God. The firmaments display his handiwork. The heavens as his creation declare and make known his power publicly. We should always think of his awesome power that brought all creation into being. Choose your thoughts wisely, exercise your authority on the earth fully. Frame your future. Living for something greater than you is satisfying. Thinking right is satisfying.

Keys on programming.
 a) *Have pictures of the future you need and think on that.*
 b) *Have scriptures that you look at and meditate on daily.*

c) Make declarations daily.
d) Replace the negative with positive thoughts.
e) Rehearse his mercies.
f) Meditate on the word.
g) Mutter the word.
h) Muse on the word.

Don't follow bad feelings and thoughts. Feelings are not reliable, they can lead you anywhere, even into the ditch. If you feel angry, you don't have to be angry necessarily. Take control over your feelings. It's easy to follow your feelings but that's the definition of indiscipline. If you follow your feelings, you will not be able to lose weight, pass examinations, go to work, study or do anything outstanding. Reign over your emotions. Many people are hurt and unlovable but we need to learn to love them. Walk in love. When you feel like not forgiving- you need to forgive. Don't follow the dictates of negative feelings. Overcome the bad feelings by not dwelling on them. Higher levels demand and attract bigger devils, so if you want to go higher, you need to master the feelings at a higher level in order to pass the tests. Don't make impulsive decisions because they come with a high price. Don't complain about what you are not ready to change. You are only ready to change things that really infuriate you. Preoccupation with the word of God can shift our attention and value system, we can begin to honor God more.

Lamentations 3:21: (This I recall to my mind, therefore have I hope.)

Recall the works of the Lord in your mind-that brings hope. Intentionally bring back from memory, recollect, remember, call or order back the thoughts that are God-based. Pursue right thoughts and the right behavior will follow suit. When Israel crossed the Jordan river, they were commanded to take some stones of remembrance from the place where they walked on. These stones were to remind them of the awesome hand of God. God had done a miracle by parting the river and this was to be recalled to mind by all the generations. The feasts of Israel were to be rehearsed on an annual basis in order to remind them of their specific relationship with God. The feast of Passover commemorates the emancipation of the Israelites from slavery in ancient Egypt. God had put in place a structure for them to be reminded of his mercies always. Don't be downcast, recall his goodness which endures forever. Make it a habit to recall his goodness. You have the power to create your daily routine that will eventually create your future. What you allow in your life and mind today, has a high likelihood of happening in your future. Change your future now-what a privilege. Americans spend about 10 billion dollars a year on therapy which in most cases can be avoided by right thinking.

Wrong thinking creates junk in your mind. Mental pollution is the introduction of contaminants into the environment of your mind that cause adverse change. Remove the pollution by substituting it with the word of God. Cherishing evil thoughts will produce evil, therefore uproot the evil thoughts. Dealing with the evil behavior is not the solution if the root is still alive and well. Deprive life from the evil thoughts. Starve them to death. Water and cultivate good thoughts. Thoughts will produce after their kind just like with physical seeds-truth is parallel. Choosing rich thoughts deliberately will create a rich default in your mind. The deliberate will lead to the automatic and subconscious thoughts. A survey was carried out on 500 billionaires and they unanimously agreed that if you think rich, you will grow rich. Thank God, I can decide to change. I can decide the direction that my thoughts will take. My mind doesn't belong to my enemy or neighbor. My mind is not for lease or rent. The flesh is a way of thinking that opposes God. We should be good custodians of our minds. Don't give room or place to the devil, he doesn't pay rent at all.

Don't think nor meditate on these negative thoughts:
- a) Anger
- b) Jealous
- c) Fear
- d) Selfishness
- e) Sadness
- f) Greediness
- g) Hate
- h) Cynicism
- i) Vengeance
- j) Stress
- k) Sarcasm
- l) Immorality
- m) Horror movies.
- n) Heartbreak movies.
- o) Gossip.
- p) Bitterness.
- q) Depressing news.
- r) Impurity
- s) Debauchery
- t) Idolatry
- u) Witchcraft
- v) Discord
- w) Rage
- x) Factions
- y) Envy
- z) Orgies

Think about these positive thoughts:
- a) Joy
- b) Abundance
- c) Goodness
- d) harmony

e) Faith
f) Gentleness
g) Faithfulness
h) Patience
i) Gratitude
j) Contentment
k) Generosity
l) Peace
m) Love
n) Faith
o) Forbearance
p) Kindness
q) Self-control
r) Multiplication
s) Blessings

Don't write-off nor condemn yourself. That's a wrong evaluation and estimation of your value. Set your mind on victory and your life will go into victory. Program your mind for success. Cause your mind to be set in the right direction and your life will go into the right direction. Apply yourself because you will not get positive results from wallowing and living self-indulgently in laziness and self-pity. Don't be in a habit of fixing outside problems but fix your thinking and the rest will fall in place.

CHAPTER TWENTY THREE

DECLARATIONS

You will never change your life until you change something you do daily. Mike Murdock

You can change your world by changing your words... Remember, death and life are in the power of the tongue. Joel Osteen

Job 22v28: (Thou shalt also decree a thing, and it shall be established unto thee: and the light shall shine upon thy ways.)

1 Chronicles 16v15 (Be ye mindful always of his covenant; the word which he commanded to a thousand generations)

Words are free but it's how you use them that may cost you. We listen to our voice more than any other voice. Speak to yourself through these decrees and declarations. If you hear something repeatedly, you will eventually believe it. These declarations will make an overall treatment to change the appearance and image of your mind. The inner dialogue of the mind is transformed. The law of sound shows us that you become what you hear. Choose what you hear. Don't listen to everything. Challenge and change the words you hear. The saints in Thessalonica were noble, because they received the word with all readiness of mind, and searched the scriptures daily. The word gives us the mind of Christ. We need the word to dig out negative thoughts that are deeply embedded in our sub-conscious mind.

We operate and function from the sub-conscious mind. Repetition of the declarations of the word of God is the key to success. Anything we repeat to our minds, we ultimately believe. What you perceive as reality becomes reality. The name Jesus appears in the Bible more than 900 times. The word Christ appears in the Bible more than 500 times. God is mentioned 4635 times in the Old and New Testaments combined. In the King James Version, the word love appears 310 times. Angels are mentioned 273 times in the Bible. The word *salvation* appears 163 times in the King James Version of the Bible. God repeats his messages to us. The message of salvation is repeated in so many ways. Right from the book of Genesis 3, the salvation picture is painted.

You have to repeat the declarations over and over again. There is power in repetition. Repetition births a belief and belief attracts miracles. The successful companies repeatedly push their messages to the customers through marketing and advertising. Repetition and consistence bring results. Take a verse that concerns your situation and repeat it over and over again. Paul admonishes us to pray without ceasing-repeatedly. We are to meditate on God's word day and night-repeatedly. Don't be against yourself. There is an internal dialogue within our minds, and that dialogue should be changed from negative to positive. If the internal conversation is negative, it leads you away from your destiny. Make your mind your servant by changing its dialogue.

Usually there is no big difference between products-the difference comes about in how that product is sold and relayed to the customers through advertising and marketing. What is said about the product changes it's value in people's eyes and minds. Minds can receive what is held before them continually. Hold the word before you continually and you will change. Remember that you are limitlessly creative, but only to the extent that you allow yourself to go. Don't be imprisoned by someone's opinion of you. Use your time wisely because no one can buy more seconds, minutes or hours. You can't carry over yesterday's 24 hours into the next day-it's use or lose it. Your thinking designs your destiny.

A principle is a law that has to be followed universally and always. Gravity is one of the laws. Every time you jump for example, you experience gravity because you are pulled back down to the ground. Without gravity, you would soar away into the atmosphere. Flying has become the norm of modern life. At any given moment in time, about five thousand airplanes are in the skies above the United States alone, equaling to an estimated 65 million commercial and private takeoffs every year. These planes use the Newton's laws of motion. The components of these laws are thrust, drag, lift and weight. It is a law that as a man thinketh so is he. To change the man, the thinking has to be changed. We have to impress good and great thoughts on our minds.

Different people react differently to the same situation because they think differently. Some see opportunities, while others see opposition in one very same instance. We reproduce according to our thought patterns. Our thought patterns produce the patterns of our lives. Your affirmations become your manifestations. If you tell yourself that you need to wake up at a certain time, you will wake up at that particular time because the mind registers it even without the use of an alarm clock. We cannot control the thoughts that are bombarded at us but we can choose the thoughts to ponder and think upon. Fill your mental storage with the word of God. The word of God heals diseased minds. The renewal of the mind by the word is of paramount importance. This renewal has to be done on a daily basis-continuous renewal. The word of God repeated enough will produce dominant thoughts and we are controlled by them. The idle mind is the devil's workshop, so keep the mind engaged into the word. God judges us for our intentions and actions. God sees our thoughts.

Genesis 3v24: So he drove out the man; and He placed at the east of the Garden of Eden the cherubim and a flaming sword which turned every way, to keep and guard the way to the tree of life.

The words from a snake in the book of Genesis ushered the evil of sin into time. Adam and Eve became naked because they believed words from the enemy. The consequences are displayed in Adam blaming Eve and Eve blaming the snake. Today humans and all creation are groaning because of the words that were shared between the first couple and the snake. Words affected their underlying beliefs, perception, covering, future, vocation, lifespan, health, descendants and promises. The snake was suggestive in misquoting of the word but Adam and Eve were gullible and their lives were never the same.

Declare and decree God's word instead of hearing from the devil. The words from a snake spoken to a man who believed them, changed the dispensation of innocence to the dispensation of conscience. After the conversation and exchange of words between man and snake, the season changed. Man began to know good and evil because of hearing negative words. Adam and Eve were driven out of Eden because of words that they admitted and accepted into their hearts.

About 6000 years later we are still witnessing the effects of believing the snake's report. The words we speak and believe can change and alter our seasons and lives. During the building of Babel, language was distorted. But when the Holy Ghost came on the day of Pentecost the language was restored. You receive what you rehearse. Make a conscious decision to speak well according to the word of God about yourself and others. Meditate on things that give you peace and not anger.

2 Timothy1v7: I declare and decree that I don't have the spirit of fear but of power, love and a sound mind.

Deuteronomy 8v18: I declare and decree that God gives me power, ideas, concepts and insights to create wealth, so that I can establish his covenant on earth.

Psalm 91v11: I declare and decree that I have angelic assistance.

Isaiah 54:17: I declare and decree that no weapon formed against me shall prosper; and every tongue that shall rise against me in judgment I shall condemn. This is the heritage of the servants of the L ORD, and their righteousness is of me, saith the L ORD.

Revelation 12v11: I declare and decree that I overcome by the blood of the Lamb, and by the word of my testimony.

Ephesians 3v20: I declare and decree that God is doing exceeding abundantly above all that i ask or think, according to the power that worketh in me.

Deuteronomy 6v10: I declare and decree that God is giving me great and goodly cities, which I did not build.

Zechariah 4v6: I declare and decree that I do exploits not by might, nor by power, but by the spirit of the L ORD of hosts.

Ephesians 1v7: I have redemption through his blood, the forgiveness of sins, according to the riches of his grace.

Ephesians 1v3: I declare and decree that I am blessed with all spiritual blessings in heavenly places in Christ:

Exodus 15v26: I declare and decree that the L ORD healeth me.

Philippians 4v19: I declare and decree that the Lord supplies all of my needs according to his riches in glory by Christ Jesus.

John 10v10: I declare and decree that I have abundant life.

James 1v5: I declare and decree that I have wisdom.

Galatians 1v4: I declare and decree that I am delivered from the evil of this present world for it is the will of God.

James 1v22: I declare and decree that I am a doer of the Word of God and I am blessed in my deeds.

Ephesians 6v16: I declare and decree that i take the shield of faith and quench every fiery dart that the wicked one brings against me.

Acts 1v8: I declare and decree that I have power.

Acts 10v38: I declare and decree that I do good.

Deuteronomy 28v2: I declare and decree that I am blessed.

Acts 4v31: I declare and decree that I am bold.

Philippians 4v13: I declare and decree that I can do all things through Christ who strengthens me.

1 Chronicles 4v10: I declare and decree that I am blessed, the hand of God is on me, my territory is enlarged, I am delivered from evil, I don't cause pain, I am honorable.

James 4v7: I declare and decree that the devil flees from me because I resist him in the name of Jesus.

Isaiah 54v13: I declare and decree that great is the peace of my children for they are taught of the Lord.

I declare and decree that I can operate a successful business.

I declare and decree that I am blessed.
I declare and decree that I am the beloved.
I declare and decree that I am a winner.
I declare and decree that I am a victor.
I declare and decree that I am prosperous.
I declare and decree that I am a property owner.
I declare and decree that I am a soul winner.
I declare and decree that my family is blessed.
I declare and decree that God loves me unconditionally.
I declare and decree that I am wise.

BIOGRAPHY

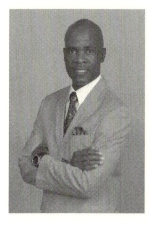

Dr Piers Finesse acquired various qualifications which include among others, an Associate Degree in Applied Sciences & a Doctorate Degree in Theology. Piers Finesse is a life-coach, an Author, a Speaker & an Entrepreneur. Piers is married to Grace & God has blessed them with two daughters and a son, Blessing, Bethany, & Bryden. He is also the Pastor of Heritage Christian Church in Mckinney Texas, USA.

Email: docdexterity@gmail.com
Piers Finesse Global Inc 2018 Production

The End

NOTES

NOTES

NOTES

NOTES

Made in the USA
Las Vegas, NV
03 February 2022

43006888R00090